A Gallery of Stars
The Story of
The Hollywood Brown Derby's
Wall of Fame

The BROWN DERBY
Restaurant
Luncheon

A Gallery of Stars

The Story of
The Hollywood Brown Derby's
Wall of Fame

by Jack Lane

Luminary Press
Baltimore, Maryland

Interior and Cover Design: Susan Svehla
Copyright © Jack Lane

Without limiting the rights reserved under the copyright above, no part of this publication may be reproduced, stored in or introduced into a retrieval system, or transmitted, in any form, or by any means (electronic, mechanical, photocopying, recording, or otherwise), without the prior written permission of the copyright owners or the publishers of this book.
ISBN 1-887664-89-0
Library of Congress Catalogue Card Number 2005923719
Manufactured in the United States of America
Printed by Thomson-Shore, Dexter, Michigan
First Printing by Luminary Press, an imprint of Midnight Marquee Press, Inc., March 2005

Acknowledgments: Bill Malin, Photofest, Buddy Weiss

Dedication

I want to thank those who helped me
manipulate this caricature concoction
all the way to the publisher.

My loving wife of 58 years,
Mitzi,
for her patience,
and my good friend,
Bill Malin,
the Super Webmaster,
who encouraged and guided me
to take the right road
without making any detours.

Table of Contents

9	Preface
10	Introduction
18	Bob Hope
26	George Burns
30	Lucille Ball and Desi Arnez
36	Ronald Reagan
40	Robert Mitchum
44	Doris Day
48	Bing Crosby
54	John Wayne
56	Groucho Marx
60	Harpo Marx
62	Bette Davis
66	Red Skelton
68	Charlton Heston
72	Judy Garland
74	Johnny Carson
76	Cary Grant
78	Clark Gable
84	Carol Burnett
88	Roy Rogers
92	Jack Paar
94	Jascha Heifetz
96	Alan Ladd
98	Ozzie and Harriet Nelson
100	Jimmy Durante
102	Sammy Davis, Jr.
104	Hollywood Hotwire
106	Milton Berle
108	Peter Lawford

112	Joe E. Brown
114	Henry Kissinger
116	Mickey Rooney
118	Norman Rockwell
120	Donald O'Connor
124	Omar Sharif
128	Danny Thomas
130	Jack Lane: The Beginning
140	Dr. Charles Lowman
142	Johnny Grant
146	Bob Feller
148	Resident Caricaturist:
149	Marjorie Rambeau
151	Louis Prima
152	Woody Herman
153	Spike Jones
154	Hedda Hopper
155	Rosalind Russell
157	Mickey Rooney
158	Eve Arden
160	Francis X. Bushman
162	Louis Jourdan
166	Victor Borge
168	Esther Williams
172	WWII
176	Edgar Bergen
178	Ernest Borgnine
180	Ray Bradbury
182	Gene Autry
186	TV Daze
191	That's a Wrap

The Original Brown Derby (Photofest)

Preface

A 56-year-old historical landmark is now history. The world-famous Hollywood Brown Derby Restaurant, the second home and launching pad for many a motion picture and television star, is no more. But happily an exact replica of the original Hollywood Brown Derby has been recreated on the grounds of the Disney-MGM Studios near Orlando, Florida.

Just about every movie idol or celebrity from any field passed through the doors of the famed Derby, and if they had reached the peak of their potential, a caricature version of their famous features was added to the Wall of Fame.

The in-house resident artist for 48 of those years and the man responsible for most of the drawings, Jack Lane, has written this book, which brings to life the charisma, the glamour, the happiness and the tears that made the Brown Derby a true Hollywood legend.

Jack traces the "growing up" of both Hollywood and the Derby down through the years. He shares many anecdotes of the stars' antics as well as events that occurred in Hollywood and especially the Brown Derby.

Hollywood, today's movie capital of the world, in addition to those glorious reels of moving entertainment, spewed forth lust, loot and Louis B. Mayer. The mass hysteria created in this setting of "Instant Money" was helped along by egos running amok, which caused the denizens of old Hollywood to run around like a horde of ants on PCP. Which of course lends itself to many interesting stories and caricatures used to illustrate this book.

The Hollywood Brown Derby had the distinction of being the first restaurant to fill their walls with famous faces. At one time, there were 800 caricatures hanging in effigy and the celebrities did everything but call their lawyers to assure themselves they had been "hung" in the right place. Hollywood stars have never been noted for being shy.

So fellow old-time film fanatic, sit back and enjoy with us this bit of nostalgic silver screen remembrances. It really is true—they had faces then.

Gary Owens poses with Jack Lane and his Sammy Davis, Jr. caricature at the Brown Derby.

Introduction

The one who came up with the title *People Are Funny* must have been God Himself. People are funny. Not funny like Bob Hope or Steve Martin funny, but funny in looks, in attitudes, in their dress, and, in general, how they screw up their role in life.

I know, because I'm in the people business, and every day I face a new crisis. I'm a caricaturist—and that is the equivalent to being a civilian paratrooper. I am fooling with peoples' *ego*! That's a dangerous proposition, sort of like counting to five when you are clutching a live three-second hand grenade in your paw.

I have so many contracts out on me that the hit men keep running into each other! Unfortunately (for me), ego was part of the package deal—human beings inherited it with everything else that was issued to us on day One. But, unfortunately most people don't know how to keep it under control. Just ask me—I'm an expert on ego. Why, do you know that in all my days on this prolific planet as an artistic witchdoctor I have operated on over 20,000 egos? That's the equivalent of a small city. If you mix that much ego together you've got yourself the most gigantic "self love-in" ever held in this country.

Hollywood movie stars hoped their caricature would make the Wall of Fame.

A great share of my pencil surgery took place at the biggest Ego Palace in the world—the Hollywood Brown Derby. If you were never lucky enough to visit the Hollywood Brown Derby, you unfortunately missed out on experiencing the birthplace of movie nostalgia. The very first meal was served on Valentine's Day 1929 and, until the Hollywood Derby closed, every show biz personality famous and infamous, well known and unknown, crossed the Derby's threshold, dined in the Derby, and, if luck, talent and fame were on their side, had their caricature placed on the Derby's Wall of Fame.

What exactly is a caricature? According to Webster's Dictionary, a caricature is "a distorted picture, exaggerated for satirical effect." But at the Hollywood Brown Derby, a caricature was a personal invitation to become a member of their "Celebrity Family." And a celebrity family it had truly been. From the first moment the Derby opened its doors, Hollywood royalty adopted it as their second home. It personified "actors in action." The stars talked—the gossip columnists stalked—and the tourists gawked. The only floorshow offered by the Derby to hungry movie fans was a view of the movie stars, who they worshiped from the altar of their local cinemas. There were so many reporters seeking interviews that press credentials were issued and columnists were given a 50 percent discount on their food bills. Derbymania prevailed. It was said that the Brown Derby was mentioned somewhere in the country 365 days a year. Fashion wars flared up at the Derby when dresses worn there by well-known actresses were "lifted" by some fashion expert and were in department store windows in Peoria, Illinois, within a week.

The Vine Street Derby was the first restaurant to put phone hookups at every table. Often the king-sized egos would have themselves paged for a phone call at their booth. They hoped that some producer, director, or agent might get their "bell rung" by the sound of the pagee's name being called. The number of calls you received at the Derby in a day gauged your Hollywood importance. One frustrated songwriter penned a song on the tablecloth, which he titled, "I've Got Those Brown Derby Nobody Called Me At Lunch Today Blues."

The Brown Derby at Hollywood and Vine

The California film capital looked upon the area of Hollywood and Vine as their very own Times Square. It really is true, "if you build it they will come." First they built movie lots and theaters and then businesses large and small followed. In the center of the hubbub of this professional population

Jack draws Charles Korvin, who portrayed the Captain in *Ship of Fools*.

explosion sat the Hollywood Brown Derby. The original restaurant building had been a studio erected by the great Cecil B. DeMille. The DeMille estate was the Derby's landlord.

The first Derby was the most famous, the one shaped like a hat, which was located on Wilshire Boulevard across from the Ambassador Hotel. In 1926, the germ of an idea was planted in the head of Herbert Somborn, who at the time was married to Gloria Swanson. The Derby was actually built to win a bet. Somborn's vanity as a businessman and food connoisseur was challenged by a close friend's quip, "If you know something about food you can sell it out of a hat..." and for many years that's just what he proceeded to do. He later sold the Brown Derby to Robert H. Cobb.

The Derby was famous for creating the Shirley Temple cocktail for Shirley Temple as well as the Cobb salad, which was created one evening by owner Robert H. Cobb.

The Hollywood Brown Derby became a reality in 1929. In 1931 the Beverly Hills Brown Derby made its debut. Located at Wilshire Boulevard and Rodeo Drive, across from the Beverly Wilshire Hotel, it, too, soon became a rendezvous for stars and society people.

Next came a Brown Derby on Los Feliz Boulevard, and a short-lived, posh restaurant called The High Hat on the corner of Wilshire and Manhattan.

Its claim to fame was based on two things—the Black Bottom Pie and the fact that Greta Garbo ate there. Nobody realized it because even in those days she was hiding out from people.

There is still a Brown Derby left today, the Orlando Derby, which is located in the heart of the Disney-MGM Studio Tour in Orlando, Florida.

The Beverly Hills Brown Derby

And whatta Derby it is! The outside is a Derby hat just as the original location. The interior is an exact replica of the Derby that was located on Hollywood and Vine. Opened in 1989, the Brown Derby in Orlando has been one of the most popular restaurants and visitors can cap off a fantastic day spent wallowing in cinematic adventures in the Disney and MGM theme parks with a grand meal and more movie memories. They find themselves dining with glorious movie stars of days gone by, who look down at them from the Brown Derby Wall of Fame. The Jack Lane caricatures of the stars bring to life those thrilling days of old-time Hollywood when men were men, women

At the Brown Derby, Mariette Hartley and Eva Marie Saint pose with Jack Lane and their caricatures.

were feisty and a kiss was just a kiss. They continue the tradition of using caricatures to honor the best in entertainment, a tradition that was started at the original Brown Derby.

In 1952, Gloria Somborn Anderson, the daughter of Gloria Swanson, took over complete control of the Derby. In 1980 she decided to call it quits and discovered she wasn't the owner of just an old hat. When word got out that this famous landmark was about to be demolished, everybody who was old enough to march got in line to carry a protest sign. The preservation groups the Los Angeles Conservancy's and the Hollywood Heritage's protests were heard loud and clear. They finally took legal action. In spite of the Andersons' complaints that they had been beset by labor strife, fires, robberies and lack of business and that they had just plain had enough, the preservation groups put a halt to the demolition. All this poor old hat wanted to do was retire.

Herbert Somborn's Hollywood Brown Derby was almost retired in its infancy by a serious fire, but instead of being a disaster it backfired into a bonanza. Somborn had a beautiful apartment right above the kitchen and over the broiler. On this particular day a grease fire started, something that could happen to anyone (if anyone cooked anymore). The flames leapt up through the apartment and the local firefighters proceeded to throw all of Somborn's high-class furniture out onto the parking lot. With the kind of luck Herb was having, the parking attendant probably charged him for "maximum time."

In spite of this attempt to emulate the "burning of Atlanta" scene in *Gone With the Wind*, the Derby managed to open its doors that evening. They had no electricity so the waiters placed a candle on each table, which probably helped age the Hollywood fire chief at least 10 years.

The next day the Herald Express had a huge banner headline: "Famous Celebrity Restaurant In Hollywood Up In Flames!!" From then on patrons flocked to the front doors, warranting management to stay open 24 hours a

Eden and Groucho Marx pose in front of some prior artists' drawings at the Brown Derby. (Photofest)

day. They adhered to this schedule for many years until the movie studios removed themselves from the true Hollywood scene. Then the Derby took the advice of Cinderella and folded at midnight before the movie hambones would turn into pumpkins.

After the Derby had been in existence about three years, a European caricaturist by the name of Vitch staggered in, made himself known, and proceeded to draw caricatures of the reigning stars, which were then hung on the more-than-ample wall space. This new approach would not only give the Derby the decoration it needed but would set it apart as the only restaurant in the nation with such a novel approach. Once the idea was conceived it developed into an ongoing project over the next 60 years. Having your caricature on the wall became a status symbol equivalent to having your foot, hand, or whatever prints placed in the concrete in front of Grauman's Chinese Theatre, or today having a star on the Walk of Fame.

Vitch did his handiwork on famous people such as Carole Lombard, William Randolph Hearst (before he could afford his castle) and others. One

You can see the caricatures lining the Derby walls in this photo. (Photofest)

of Vitch's outstanding efforts for the Derby walls was a study of Franklin Delano Roosevelt, where he took the initials F.D.R. and, by clever manipulation, maneuvered those three letters into a face that was, without a doubt, F.D.R. It was the biggest of all the drawings on the wall and, as a result, hung directly over the main entrance. There was only one problem—it hung there under protest. It just so happened that Bob Cobb, then President of the Brown Derby Corporation, was a rabid Republican, and F.D.R. wasn't exactly his idea of Superman. However, there was probably a hole in the wall at that point and the "Prez's" picture covered it nicely, so up it stayed. That is until F.D.R. was officially no longer among us and that picture came *down* but *fast*!

After a period of time, Vitch left the Derby and the U.S. and went to Europe to join the Polish Army and the French underground, which only goes to show how dangerous he thought Hollywood was!

After trying the efforts of several local caricaturists, Cobb got hold of me in Chicago to come out and replace Vitch. When I got to the Derby I told everyone I was the "Son of Vitch." Upon my arrival, I was overwhelmed by the tremendous conglomeration of caricatures on the walls, each hanging in

Kay Kyser strikes a pose for me at the Brown Derby.

its own frame loosely, and each, by its askew position on the wall, indicating the strength of last night's earthquake tremor.

Many folks have asked who was the first celebrity I ever drew—I tell them in jest I was sitting in a theater drawing Abraham Lincoln when the bullet whizzed by my ear. I had done one of John Wilkes Booth the week before and he was aiming at me and missed and hit Lincoln.

The first celebrity I was asked to sketch at the Derby was Bob Burns, a down home comedian from Arkansas who played the bazooka, which was a homemade horn-type instrument he had invented. His invention was so popular WWII soldiers nicknamed their new shoulder-held rockets after the zany horn, and so today the term bazooka automatically calls to mind a rocket launcher. At the time Burns was a co-star on the *Bing Crosby Radio Show* and Paramount's answer to Will Rogers. Bob was very genteel, and he only hit me over the head with the bazooka once after seeing my effort. Since that time, I make a standing offer to anyone I draw—if they don't like what they see, I'll meet them in small claims court. Of course, the stars didn't have a chance because my lawyer was Perry Mason—and he never lost a case. He lost his TV series, but he never lost a case.

BOB HOPE

One of the frequent visitors to the Derby was another guy who never lost—lost a chance to get a smile out of someone that is—Bob Hope. Of course, that was the name of the game for Bob. Having people laugh with him was what kept his blood circulating. Who needs vitamins when a good hearty laugh will bring the same results?

If it hadn't been for Charlie Chaplin, Bob might not have been where he was. He could have still been a golf caddy, which is what he started out doing. Of course, if you loved golf the way Bob did, that wouldn't have been all that bad—although there would have been a little difference in his income tax bracket.

As a kid, Hope loved going to the movies and he became a one-man Chaplin fan club. He was such a fan, he began to imitate him on any occasion. Bob was doing such a dead on impersonation that his six brothers entered him in a Charlie Chaplin Imitation Contest, which he won. In later years, Hope's nose was put out of joint because he learned from Walt Disney that as a kid Walt had also won a Charlie Chaplin contest at the Kansas City Rialto Theatre. Walt's prize was two whole dollars. All Bob had received for his win was applause and an overdose of heckling from his brothers.

The most dangerous aspect of Hope's life was when he changed his name to "Packy East" and proceeded to enter the prizefighting ring. They weren't wearing nose guards in those days so he was really taking his life in his hands. He had an unusual style—he didn't jab with his left or his right hand, he jabbed with the end of his nose. When the other fighters began to leave their glove prints all over it, Hope decided to stick his nose into some other business.

In the evening after high school classes in Cleveland, Bob had learned to tap dance. When he learned Fatty Arbuckle was appearing on a vaudeville bill in his hometown, Hope acquired a partner, Lloyd Durbin, and they put together a dance routine and became a cheap act for the Arbuckle run. They moved around the stage a lot so they wouldn't make too easy of a target. The two of them played the Gus Sun Circuit for the smart amount of $40 a week, but it gave them enough to buy new shoelaces for their tap shoes and the daily newspaper to see how their act was doing in the reviews. At one time they joined a road show where they danced, did a blackface act and Hope played the saxophone. When he got threatening letters from Rudy Vallee he gave up the sax. In the meantime he was branching out into comedy monologues and, as they weren't burning down the theaters after his

performances, he decided to go it alone as a comedian. Vaudeville agents had more than their share of would-be comedians, so they weren't exactly standing in line to book him.

A square meal was beginning to become just a dim memory when he got a booking at the Stratford Theatre in Chicago. It was supposed to be a Friday through Sunday engagement but Hope was hungry and managed to stretch it into six months. When I was talking to him, I mentioned that I was the only other emcee who had been held over at the Stratford Theatre but I only lasted two weeks because I ran out of material. He said, "Are you kidding? The only thing that kept me going was, I would get every gag I could from the acts on the bill this week so I could tell them in the show next week." (You see he had gag writers even then but they didn't get paid!) Some of the jokes were in dialect and Bob said he murdered them...and when you stop to think of it, had you ever heard Hope do a gag in dialect? I guess he learned his lesson when the musicians in the pit at the Stratford threw their chairs onto the stage at him.

Bob had his first Hollywood screen test in 1930 but he made one mistake...he didn't bring Bing Crosby and Dorothy Lamour with him. He did his current vaudeville act. After waiting a week to hear from his agent, he called him and asked how he had done. It was the wrong question because the answer came back, "Do you really want to know?" Hope refused to believe it was that bad, so he went to see the test himself. The agent was right...it *was* bad.

So it was back to vaudeville and an eventual rise to the top rung when he played The Palace in New York. Since he was now on Broadway, he decided to stay there. He just changed theaters to do the musicals, *Ballyhoo* and *Roberta*. Bob was the hit of the show in *Roberta*, stealing it from some pretty good pros such as Sydney Greenstreet, Fred MacMurray and George Murphy. This time, Hollywood called Hope, but he was doing so well in the musical and making some radio appearances, as well as hav-

BOB HOPE

R-K-O PALACE, NEW YORK

Now—Week Feb. 21

BOOKED SOLID R-K-O

Direction, LEE STEWART

ing an offer to do some comedy shorts in the New York film industry, his answer to Hollywood was, "Who needs you?" He did his first short in New York for Educational Pictures. When he went to the theater to see the finished product, he was ready to turn himself in to the law for imitating an actor. Hope met Walter Winchell outside the theater and Winchell, not having seen the film, said, "How was it?" Hope replied, "I'll tell you how it was. When they catch John Dillinger they're going to make him sit through it, *twice*." Good old Winchell put Bob's crack in his column verbatim, and when the producer read it he gave Hope's option a Watergate shredding.

Jane Russell and Shirley MacLaine help Bob Hope celebrate Christmas in 1958.

These were just minor detours along the road to success for Bob Hope. You know Hope, when he decided to go somewhere, he was going to get there. He did enough radio spots to earn his own show, which was sponsored by Pepsodent. He surrounded himself with good writers and good people in the show. Between Skinnay Ennis, the bandleader, and the fabulous comic, Jerry Colonna, plus a teenaged girl singer by the name of Judy Garland, Hope's show skyrocketed.

Hollywood swung the door open wide this time and Hope made par on his first picture, *The Big Broadcast of 1938*. Later, the *Road* pictures with Bing Crosby and Dorothy Lamour made entertainment history and, oh, what history they made.

In the next few years, Bob had more flight time than anyone in the United States Air Force. He played so many military bases that at times he wasn't sure whether they were theirs or ours. If he went into the mess hall and was served chow mein he knew his navigator had goofed. When you were in the service if you were having trouble with your stomach, or your back, or

a wound you went to the infirmary to see the Doc, but if your morale needed some lifting, you just waited 'til Bob Hope and Company got to your camp.

Bob's home was so loaded with trophies, plaques, awards and citations that Dolores had to have a road map to find her way to the bathroom. Oscar is the only award that eluded

Bob on a USO Christmas tour in Southeast Asia, 1966

him, but then who would want something named Oscar in their home? That's a dog's name. (And a lot of times that's who it is awarded to.) Actually, Bob did take home several awards from the Academy including Honorary Awards in 1941, 1945, 1953 and 1966, and in 1960 he received the Jean Hersholt Humanitarian Award. Among Bob's most memorable achievements was the honor of being voted into the Living Hall of Fame at the Smithsonian Institution.

Bob wasn't kidding when he sang, *"Thanks for the Memories"* because he was thankful for his own memory that was an encyclopedia of jokes. He more than likely helped Joe Miller write the first gag. One of Hope's biggest thrills was when Paulette Goddard introduced her husband, Charlie Chaplin, to him. This was not the imitator; this was the imitatee! When Charlie said, "Hope, you are one of the best timers of comedy I've ever seen," it was equivalent to Woody Hayes telling someone on his squad, "You're a damned good football player."

Thanks for the memories

Silent film diva Mae Murray

In my 42 years at the original Brown Derby, I have had the pleasure (and the nerve) to distort and defame some of the most famous profiles in Hollywood history, and, to add insult to injury, hang them in effigy on the wall. Can you imagine being hung between such villains as Peter Lorre and Boris Karloff? There never was such a thing as "protocol on the wall." Where you lands is where you stays—and this fact often led to a few temper tantrums.

I'll never forget my first unveiling—40 new faces to replace 40 who had defended their squatter's rights to the wall with fervor. It was "in between" time at the Derby—in between lunch and dinner, and the place was devoid of patrons with the exception of a couple of snack fans and one woman hovering over her hot tea. The waiters and hired hands were busy moving or retiring some pictures, and I was on hand to see where my victims' caricatures landed, so I could come up with the all-important answer to the critical question, "Where am I hung?" Suddenly, there was a scream and everyone scrambled to the table of the little lady, certain that the hot tea had taken up residence in her lap. It turned out to be even more crucial. The little lady identified herself in her haughtiest manner as the famous silent film star, Mae Murray. The reason for the loud-sounding scream from a silent film star was that she had just discovered her caricature, one that had hung on the front wall of the Derby for 15 years, was missing. This called for drastic action! Every able-bodied man on the Derby payroll went on a picture-to-picture hunt for Miss Murray's visage.

Finally, it was discovered that she had been moved to the back wall and was hanging over the bar. This was the blow fatale! Mae threatened to call her studio, cussed out owner Bob Cobb, and swore she would never grace the Derby premises again. Her performance didn't win her an Oscar, but it did get her back on the front wall. Hanging around a bar is one thing, but hanging over one is for the birds.

On that same occasion, the intent was to remove some of the faces of those who had taken up permanent residence in Forest Lawn. Among those unfortunates was Wallace Beery, who had been gone for a number of years (he

Wallace Beery

passed away April 15, 1949). When word got out that he was soon to be retired from the wall, there was so much steam raised you would have thought that the main plant at Sauna Baths, Inc., had sprung a leak. So Wallace Beery stayed, and of course, with good reason. He had served his apprenticeship in the very earliest of movies and by the time he landed at Metro-Goldwyn-Mayer, he was second only to Lionel Barrymore in longevity in the acting ranks. His teaming with Marie Dressler in *Min and Bill* (MGM, 1930) made Mutt and Jeff and Toots and Casper take a back seat for laughs in this dark comedy/drama. Wally won critical praise for his acting, and earned an Academy Award for Best Actor for *The Champ* (1932; he tied with Fredric March for *Dr. Jekyll and Mr. Hyde*). *The Champ* also received the first award in international competition in the Venice Film Festival. In 1934, he won the Venice Film Festival Special Recommendation for his portrayal of Pancho Villa in *Viva Villa*. Other pictures that won the fans' applause were *Grand Hotel* and *Dinner at Eight*. Dinner wasn't always at eight the nights he ate at the original Brown Derby.

Other patrons who became the first Derby devotees were Mary Pickford, Bebe Daniels, Louella Parsons and Loretta Young,

By the time I had given a facelift to the Hollywood Brown Derby's hallowed walls by introducing current personalities among the old establishment of stars, there were more than 800 sketches to be ogled by all.

GEORGE BURNS

One of the celebs who rated two caricatures in my book was George Burns—his career spanned several generations and was more than worthy of two frames. The first sketch he sat for me was in 1947. When I did the second one he was bearing down hard on 90. George's nickname as a kid was "Nattie," although his official name was Nathan Birnbaum. Even though he was the ninth of 12 children, he broke away from the pack and made a big name for himself.

He started his legendary career in vaudeville as a stand-up comedian, but when he later teamed with Gracie Allen, he became a straight man for Gracie's winsome witticisms. His comedic talent was in the background as he helped writers come up with Gracie's zany dialogue. Theirs were one of the only shows to make the successful transition from radio to television, and they managed to keep their ratings high for the next eight years. They were nominated three times for Emmys for *The George Burns and Gracie Allen Show* (1950-1958) for the best comedy series, and Gracie was nominated six times for the best actress and comedienne award. George invented a "first" on their show when he would stop in the middle of shooting and would step out of character to kibitz with the audience and then move back into the set. When Gracie passed away George moved on with his life, but he stayed devoted to Gracie. He was often seen with younger women, but he always complained, "I'd go out with women my age but there are no women my age." When he was in his 80s, he made the film *Oh, God!* Roger Ebert in his review noted, "The casting of George Burns as God is an inspiration." At the ripe old age of 80 he won the Best Supporting Actor Award for his performance in

GEORGE BURNS

The Sunshine Boys with Walter Matthau. He became the oldest male actor to ever win an Oscar.

He didn't kid around with the famous places he went and was seen. Spago's, Chasen's, The Pantages Theatre, Disneyland, many times in the Hollywood Christmas Parade, and the Academy Awards. He had a star on the Walk of Fame and his footprints at Mann's Chinese Theatre. Everyplace he went he had his perpetual cigar, but he never dropped an ash at any of them. I just knew the cigar I drew in his mouth in 1947 was exactly the same cigar he was smoking in 1987.

I have always contended you are going to go nowhere in the age bracket unless you have a sense of humor. George Burns and Bob Hope died at age 100, Milton Berle at 93 and Victor Borge at 91, pretty good proof that humor keeps you young. It's not exactly fun getting old, but if you have smiled and laughed a lot in your life, the trip wasn't all that bad.

Gracie Allen in 1939

LUCILLE BALL AND DESI ARNEZ

Very, very few big theatrical stars can say they got their first start on Broadway as a soda jerk. No, not in a play—but for real! Lucille Ball could lay claim to that one and you gotta admit she was the most famous soda jerk in the world.

This were was her period of odd jobs, which anyone in show biz has to go through in order to provide the bod with some calories. Lucy could blame her love of performing on the vaudeville shows and early movies she used to see as a kid. She would head home and immediately act out all the parts and the routines for her mother. As any nurturing mother will do, she encouraged Lucille and that was all Lucy needed. She proceeded to take over her high school shows by producing, directing, casting, building the sets and even hauling in the props.

Little did she know that that was exactly what she would be doing later at Desilu Productions. This initial success encouraged her to head for New York and enroll in drama school at the age of 15. She was a little overwhelmed by the star pupil, Bette Davis, and her boyfriend, "Petuh, Petuh, Petuh," so after six weeks she was sent back home because of her shyness. It was probably the only time in Lucille Ball's life that she ever gave up. She returned to high school until she earned the fare to return to New York. She had a hunch her name was agin' her, so she changed it to Diane Belmont. The change at least got her hired for two big shows, Earl Carroll's Vanities and Shubert's Stepping Stones, but before they opened, she had to close when they fired her.

Modeling at Hattie Carnegie's elegant dress salon and freelancing for some of the top commercial photographers and magazine illustrators such as McClelland Barclay were next on the agenda. Things were beginning to hum, but then she found out that the humming was coming from her rheumatoid arthritis and this little session cost her two years of her life.

She finally got the show on the road when she posed as the Chesterfield Cigarette Girl on a nationwide campaign. This was before the "no smoking" signs showed up all over the world, so she did get good exposure. It looked like her career was really smoking when she was selected as one of the Goldwyn girls in the Eddie Cantor film, *Roman Scandals*. Lucy thought she was in like Flynn as far as Hollywood was concerned, but Errol Flynn had a corner on the market. The best Lucy could do were 10 bit film parts and she did not even receive billing. Even then she felt she was more of a comedienne,

Bob and Sally Cobb, owners of The Brown Derby, with Lucille Ball and Desi Arnez

so she joined up with the best of them at the time, Leon Errol and the Three Stooges, and made two-reel comedies and had some bit parts in five full-length pictures. This won her her next title, "Queen of the B's," as she worked out a seven-year contract at RKO. She finally rebelled and announced to them, "I'm not going to work as a show girl in the background anymore."

Her next 22 pictures over a period of six years were just about as unrewarding. Since she spent so much time in the background, she had time to check out the scenery in one of her pictures and discovered Desi Arnez. Desi's number one profession at the time was as a bongo-playing bandleader, an unbeatable combination to say the least. Lucy found the movie biz so disenchanting she turned to radio and quickly accepted a role as the scatterbrained wife in the CBS show, *My Favorite Husband*. Previously she had made appearances on the Phil Baker show and on Jack Haley's program.

Just to prove that she was coming into her own in the world of slapstick, Lucille was the instigator of an incident that occurred in the Hollywood Brown Derby and it's a shame it wasn't on film. Lucy was sitting at her Derby booth with Gene Lester, the Derby photographer and another gentleman, when she spied her coworker on the radio show, Jack Haley, who was sitting clear across the dining room. The Derby always served a basket of hard rolls with luncheon. Ball first tried to get Haley's attention by signaling him, but when that didn't work she decided to use more efficient methods. She took one of the hard rolls, stood up on the seat, and flung it across the room at Jack. As the roll barely missed him, Haley took cover, sure that some irate fan who didn't like his last show was out to do him in. After a quick eyeballing of the room to see where the next baked hand grenade was coming from (he had already been the recipient of three), he spotted Lucy winding up like Dizzy Dean and preparing to throw her best slider. With that he grabbed one of his rolls and let fly at Lucy. From then on it was open warfare. The only thing that saved the Derby from being sued by someone getting hit in the noggin by a flying sourdough was the fact that it was after the luncheon crowd had made its exit and there were few targets left. Chillious, the Derby maitre d',

William Frawley, Lucy and William Holden at The Hollywood Brown Derby when *I Love Lucy* went to Hollywood.

was horrified at the obstacle course that was beginning to pile up in the aisle, but he knew the busboys still had to have their inning and although he would have a tough time explaining this dough debacle to them, especially in Spanish, he knew they would sweep the plate.

In 1947 when I went to her table to draw her she said, "You can only do a caricature of me if you do one of my boyfriend," who was sitting at the table. This was some guy named Desi Arnez. I had never heard of him and I'm sure, outside of his relatives, no one else knew of him. But I did the two of them and they both got up on the wall.

She trod the boards of the legitimate theater still looking for the chance to expose her sense of comedy.

At Bob Hope's request she journeyed over to Paramount, where she did a couple of movies (*Sorrowful Jones*, 1949 and *Fancy Pants*, 1950) with Hope, but she was beginning to develop an acute case of frustrationitis. She felt so positive that she, an American redhead, and Desi, a Cuban bandleader with an accent so heavy it sounded like he carried his bongo drum around in his mouth, could become a comedy team that would be a grabber as far as the viewing public was concerned. To persuade the CBS higher-ups they had an act, Lucy and Desi toured vaudeville theaters doing three or four skits in a

20-minute span. They proved their point and were offered a half-hour situation comedy series playing the part of Ricky and Lucy Ricardo, who had friends and neighbors Fred and Ethel Mertz. This was the only part of the format that was suspect. How could your "best friends" also be your landlords? This all had to be before rent control.

They set television on its ear in more ways than one. By presenting the episodes in sequence à la a play, performing before a live audience and using a three-camera technique to film the show while doing it live, they started a whole new thing. Within their first six months, *I Love Lucy* was rated TV's number one show. Lucille ended up doing 156 *I Love Lucy* shows and at least 144 *Here's Lucy*, plus many, many specials and spectaculars. We all say, "thank you, thank you" for her efforts as we daily enjoy the reruns of her hilarious hijinks. She taught us all how important it is to laugh.

Vivian Vance and Lucille Ball on the set of *I Love Lucy*

In Desi Arnez' autobiography *A Book* (1976), he gave Lucille "90 percent of the credit" for the tremendous success of the *I Love Lucy* show. The worldwide acclaim they received over the years included being nominated for an Emmy 23 times and actually winning five. This places their show in good company in the top 10—the other top winners are *Fraiser*, *The Mary Tyler Moore Show* and *Cheers*. Proving once again that the average Joe and Josephine need a good laugh when they are fed up with jobs, housework, misbehaving kids and just want to sit down, relax, and have a few laughs that might help salvage a long hard day. *Milton Berle's Texaco Show*, *The Beverly Hillbillies*, and *All in the Family* were also in that distinguished group.

Lucy even stole the welcome mat out from under President Dwight D. Eisenhower when more people watched little Ricky's birth on *I Love Lucy* than watched Ike's inauguration. That should have taught all future Presidents that you don't try to buck the top show on the air for attention. Lucy and Desi were everyone's favorite life of the party.

RONALD REAGAN

My first exposure to the newest vanity breakthrough, contact lenses, came while drawing a guy who, to this day, probably wasn't ever suspected of needing them. I had drawn him at the Derby when he was about the most popular star on the Warner Bros. lot. By the time I got my second crack at his famous profile, he had become the head of the Screen Actors Guild. It just so happened that Janie Powell was having a party that included many Hollywood celebs and I was called upon to wield my pulverizing pencils until the time the caterers took over by wielding their sizzling steak knives. My victim was sitting in front of me and taking his pencil beating like a man as the other guests stood around giving him a verbal caricature, as friends are wont to do.

He got to laughing so hard at their jibes that he had to stop me, as my drawing hand was in mid-air. He grabbed a handkerchief from his pocket, threw his head forward twice, and then started rubbing something that was in the handkerchief. I had no idea what he was doing, with all this rapid-fire action, I thought the guy was having an epileptic seizure—and he hadn't even seen the drawing yet. After wiping his eyes, he cupped his hand, threw back his head twice and blinked. I finally realized I had just been a witness to the first act of "you have just come in contact with a contact." The personality was Ronald Reagan, who in due time, dropped the "Mister" from in front of his name in favor of "President."

1942 studio portrait

Many a time at the annual White House Easter Egg Hunt, Ronald would be seen groping on the ground while looking for his contact so he could see enough to begin the egg hunt. Imagine what would

Virginia Mayo and Ronald Reagan in 1948

have happened if as president he had lost one of his contacts just as he was going to press the red panic button!

In the early days of his career Reagan pounded the pavement in Chicago trying to get an announcer's job but all he got was the same old lick "go out and get yourself some experience." At an interview at WOC in Davenport he said as he was heading for the door, "It doesn't look as if I'll ever get to be a sports announcer." The director said, "Why didn't you say you were a sports announcer?" "I'm not," said Ronnie, "I only want to be one."

Those words were repeated in 1976 when a kid asked him if he was the President and he reiterated, "I'm not. I only want to be one." Reagan spent four years broadcasting the big athletic events of the day from major league baseball to Big Ten football, to the Drake Relays. It was while he was covering spring training at Catalina for the Chicago Cubs that the California sunshine ricocheted off his skull and he got the urge to be an actor. A friend

Ronald Reagan (right) 1931

suggested he take off his glasses, which at that point he had worn so much they looked as though they were painted on. She also gave him the name of an agent who called Warner Bros. and arranged for a screen test. Another test was on the next day's agenda, but Ron, known as "Dutch Reagan," had a ballgame he had to cover, and with the loyalty of a Vin Scully running through his blood, he took off for Des Moines. Thanks to the bike that carried the Western Union message boy to his door, Reagan got the message "Warners is offering you a contract." "Grab it before they change their minds," was Ronnie's response.

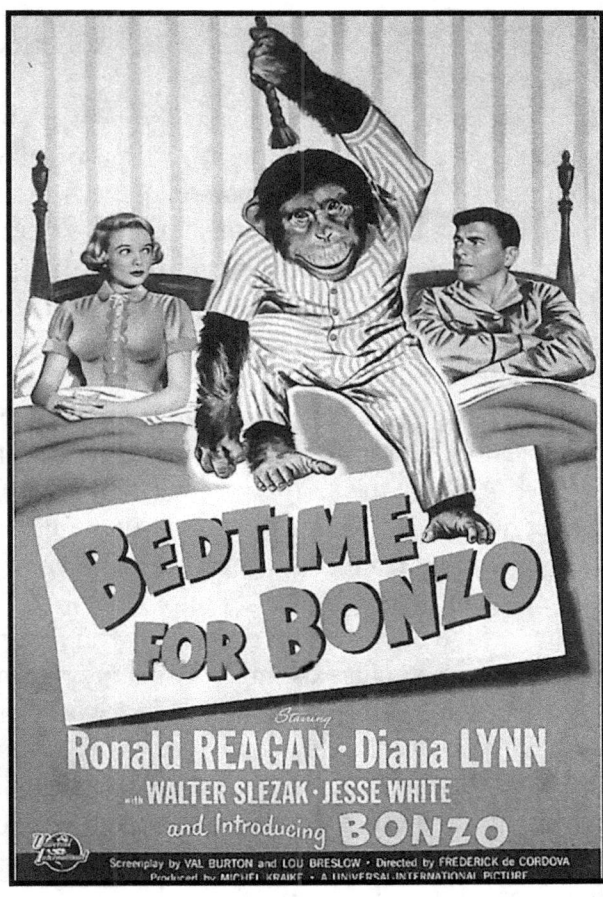

His first assignment was as a radio commentator in a B picture, *Love Is On the Air* (1937). Ron had prepared himself (as he always did in whatever he undertook to do) for a future as an actor by studying dramatics in both high school and college. He was also big on athletics in school, having played football and been a swimming coach.

Warner Bros. was really giving Reagan a workout making films when the Army stepped in and beckoned him to active duty. When he was discharged three and one half years later he held the rank of Captain. He climbed right back up the popularity poll both in Hollywood and at the box office. In 1947 he returned to the old alma mater, Eureka College in Illinois, and "Dutch" got the full celebrity treatment with the parades, the welcome signs, the enthusiasm, and the opportunity to sportscast one more football game for the home team.

Incidentally, this caricature of Reagan is his high school graduation picture. Remember, it was sketched in 1947!

ROBERT MITCHUM

"You know you can't act, and if you hadn't been good looking you would never have gotten a picture. I'm tired of playing with people who have nothing to offer." This was a direct quote from the feisty Katharine Hepburn and the target for her tongue-lashing was Robert Mitchum. However, down through the years, the critics didn't exactly go along with Katy's blasting. They said he had "easy, physical grace," "an effortless style," "his is a grand performance, which showed a mixture of vigor and tenderness," and in 1945, he earned a nomination for an award of the Academy of Motion Picture Arts and Sciences as the best supporting actor of the year.

The nomination came about for his performance in *The Story of G.I. Joe* (United Artists); the script was based on the writings of every GI's favorite war correspondent, Ernie Pyle. So Mitchum proved that he had a little more going for him than just the good looks. In spite of the fact that he was never the recipient of a high school diploma, Bob got himself into gear by being a writer, which only goes to prove that you don't have to be too smart to put words on paper. (Just ask me!) His first crack at it was as a ghostwriter for the astrologer, Carroll Richter. I guess when you're talking about "celestial bodies" you have to be a ghostwriter. When he got up to Scorpio, he ended his tour with Richter. Mitchum tried to make the grade writing for radio, but somewhere along the line, he was missing out on the usual number of meals, so he started punching the clock at Lockheed Aircraft Corporation. If you think the electronic sonic booms of a rock band are ear shattering, you ain't heard nuthin' til your eardrums are exposed to the noise of the machinery in an aircraft factory. It sounds like the Army and Air Force are all inside the building at the same time and revving their motors all over the place.

When Bob found that he was

talking to himself and he had to yell to hear what he was saying, he decided he had had enough. He tried selling shoes but he found the women were noisier than the machinery had been when it came to trying to find something they liked that they could still manage to squeeze all of their toes into. His lifesaver was a booking agent who introduced him to William Boyd, better known as Hopalong Cassidy. Boyd took one look at the discontented face of this fugitive from noisy machines and madams and hired him as a villain for his next picture. Mitchum didn't know when he was well off because now he had to learn to ride a horse. How many Western movies have you ever seen where the cowboy jogs alongside the horse? He made seven more *Hopalong Cassidy* films before he finally got rid of the horse, which had been stealing most of the scenes anyway.

Robert Mitchum in *Till the End of Time* (1945)

In 1944 Bob signed a contract with RKO Radio Pictures and by 1946, the Motion Picture Herald named him one of the "Stars of Tomorrow" in its national poll. They knew what they were talking about. In 1960 Mitchum was named by the National Board of Review Best Actor for his roles in *Home From the Hill* (MGM) and *The Sundowners* (Warner Bros.).

For a guy who couldn't act, he played just about every type of part that the film industry could come up with. And to think he did it all just to prove to Katharine Hepburn she didn't know what she was talking about. He knew he was going to be a successful actor because he had read it in one of Carroll Richter's horoscopes (which Mitchum had written himself!)

DORIS DAY

Back in the dark ages when I graduated from high school, I got myself into show biz. Thanks to an imitation of Joe Penner and his duck (I don't know which I did best) [Joe Penner was a 1930s radio comic known for saying "Wanna buy a duck?" and his laugh], Rudy Vallee and his megaphone, and F.D.R. and his fireside chat, I was able to tour the vaudeville circuit. In one of the towns in Michigan, I was on the same bill as Barney Rapp and his orchestra, featuring a girl singer by the name of Doris Day. Doris was quite young in those days, as was I, so we were very compatible. Between shows we would go out to dine and after the last show, go out someplace to have a Coke so we wouldn't have to show our I.D. cards. On any of these occasions, her Mama was always along to protect Doris's bod. Doris was a real nice gal and had a great voice even then. Her goal in life was to be a dancer, but when she had a serious accident that affected her legs, she took up singing…and, it was just as well she did. As your ears will tell you, she made a ballad sound as though was written just for you and your lover.

But time marches on. Doris eventually wound up with the Les Brown Band and on the Bob Hope radio show, and I made the giant leap from vaudeville into one of Uncle Sam's ill-fitting uniforms. The next time I saw Doris Day was when she came into the Derby with a famous movie director, Michael Curtiz, who had just completed his 45th film. The studio was grooming Doris for stardom. Little did I know that that meant, "Forget everything and anybody you knew in the past." As I sat to do her caricature, I was so elated at seeing her again. I started rehashing all the fun we had had and good times in the Barney Rapp

Doris Day poses for me as Michael Curtiz watches.

days. I suddenly felt I had opened a refrigerator door by mistake. Icicles began to form on the end of my nose from the quick freeze I was getting. It was then I realized that once you "get into the movies," everyone beneath that level becomes a member of the leper colony.

I had one other meeting with Doris when it became obvious this thing was getting the best of her. The night I drew her husband, Marty Melcher, her manager at the time, the three of us sat in the booth, Doris, myself in the middle, then Marty. As I'm doing my sketch, a friend of Marty's stops in the aisle and greets him warmly. Marty says to him, "I'd like you to meet my wife, Doris Day." Doris, who is shoveling the food into her face, glances up quickly, says "Hi," and goes back to the task at hand. After the gentleman finished his conversation with Marty, he moved further into the dining room and sat down. Marty turns on Doris and said, "Whatzamatter with you! Why didn't you talk to that guy? He's a friend of mine." Doris snapped back, "I said 'hi,' didn't I?" I finished that drawing fast and got out of the middle of what was shaping up as a Tong war (or is it "tongue" war?).

Later the book she wrote about herself, Doris Day, Her Story, completely altered her girl-next-door image. I felt vindicated in my feeling that she had changed considerably from the days when "I knew her when."

BING CROSBY

One of the most clever publicity stunts ever pulled off was by a record company plugging a "to be released the next day" Bing Crosby record. One night, as soon as the Derby closed its doors for the evening, the PR people from the record company began the horrendous task of taking down every one of the 800 framed pictures, removing the drawings, putting Bing Crosby's caricature in each one and rehanging them before dawn. When you walked in for lunch that day, you thought you had a Crosby hangover—all you could focus on was Bing!

Of course a lot of the public got to focus on Bing; he would frequently drop into the Derby since it was so close to the radio studio.

Bing sang from the time he was a young pup. Talk about singing at the drop of a hat, he needed no encouragement. A little applause and he would break into another medley. He sang his way in and out of Gonzaga University in Spokane, Washington and into the local pubs. Along the way he tied in with Al Rinker, who was the brother of the popular blues singer, Mildred Bailey. He and Al hit the vaudeville trail, which was then the proving ground for all talent. It proved to be their *im*proving ground when they were asked to audition for and were signed up by orchestra leader Paul Whiteman.

They weren't exactly laying the audiences in the aisles, so Whiteman brought a third member into the group, Harry Barris, and called the trio The Rhythm Boys.

At this point Whiteman's band was pretty much of a roving band of alcoholics, an environment that was no help to Bing. Their dictum was anything for a laugh. The very first night Whiteman introduced jazz violinist Joe Venuti to a Carnegie Hall audience, Joe came out, playing the fiddle, astride a big white milk horse. Pandemonium set in. Whiteman was no slouch in the anti-freeze department either. Venuti had just completed building a new home in Long Island and invited the band to the grand opening house warming. The evening came to a slam-dunk when Whiteman stood up on a chair, lit a newspaper, and set fire to Joe's brand new beamed ceiling. Hardly what is meant by house warming! It cost Joe a new roof but it was FUN! Crosby's association with Whiteman's orchestra exposed him to some of the best musicians of the time. The musicians loved him because he always sang on pitch. Bing didn't play an instrument but he had a terrific ear for music (actually two, and they were king sized).

He learned the riffs that made Bix Beiderbecke and the Dorseys such geniuses at their trade. For Crosby it wasn't a matter of just singing a song,

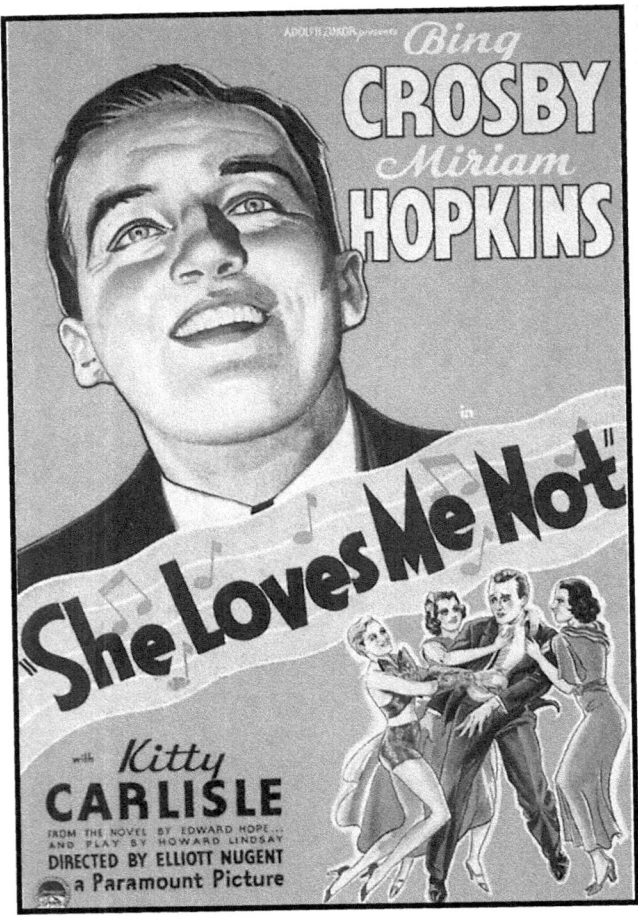

he wanted to phrase it so it wasn't just so many words, but rather that it had some musical content. His vocal skills moved him out of the title of the "first Big Band singer," to a recording break with Gus Arnheim at the Cocoanut Grove. Instant popularity on radio followed. It was all coming up roses—and fast! Movies became a must and in just two years he was Paramount's biggest box office attraction. One word could describe all of Bing's pictures—enjoyable!

The fact that a toupee had to be added to make his physical appearance more cinema friendly in no way marred his appeal with the public. Bing thought so little of the rug that occasionally he would sit at the bar at the Brown Derby without the hairpiece and no one would peg him. At one of his radio shows, the outstanding photographer, Gene Lester, came in to shoot a series of candid shots at the rehearsal for the J. Walter Thompson Advertising Agency. A New York publicist asked Gene to say hello to Bing for him. Gene introduced himself, passed on the friend's regards, which Bing acknowledged and appreciated. "However," he said, "You can't take pictures of me today because I don't have my toupee or my hat with me." Gene said, "Don't worry Bing, I've got the problem all solved." He reached into his camera case and pulled out a flash bulb about the size of a 150-watt bulb. He had previously cut some brown, fuzzy hair off of a rug, glued it on top of the bulb, and parted it in the middle. "See Bing," he said, "Knowing the circumstances, I'm using flash bulbs with hair on 'em!" When Bing stopped guffawing he said, "To hell with it. Take any picture you want."

Songwriters who were striving to make their tunes an automatic hit were constantly besieging Bing to be the first to sing the new song—because he could sing anything and make it a hit. Ballads, the blues, hymns and country—all became a happening when Bing took over the vocal reins. He made it all sound so easy. He was an inspiration to every guy and gal giving vocalization to his or her interpretation of the song. Some people gave up taking baths just so they could stand in the shower and "sing like Bing." These showerbound wannabes would, along with Bing, be crooning some of the best music around from top movies such as *Holiday Inn*, *Going My Way* and *Here Comes the Groom*—all springboards for Oscar-winning songs. "In the Cool, Cool of the Evening" by the two greats, Johnny Mercer and Hoagy Carmichael, "Would You Like To Swing On A Star" by Burke and Van Heusen, and "White Christmas" by Irving Berlin all garnered Best Song trophies. Between the record sales, the royalties and the radiant regard for "White Christmas," the song may soon replace the National Anthem.

With Bing's record sales (well over 500 million) and the tremendous box office success of most of his movies, he could very well have turned into the egomaniac of the century. No way! He was overwhelmed by it all, but he graciously took it in stride. He had a 10-year span of being voted most popular film actor and during that time he was chosen as the most recognizable person in the world.

He always had one advantage over Bob Hope, and that was probably the source for much heckling. Bing won the coveted Oscar for his stellar performance in

51

Hope and Crosby on *The Road to Hong Kong*

Going My Way. His concept of a goodly priest who actually seemed a down-to-earth human being, who played baseball, wore sweatshirts and was never holier than thou won him acclaim from both the public and the religious order. Bing was almost ordained a priest by Pope Pius XII because he was so enthused with Bing's portrayals in both *Going My Way* and *The Bells of St. Mary's*. Who says Bing couldn't act! Crosby's religious upbringing came to the fore when he donated all of the royalties from the record-selling recording of "Silent Night" to charity. These were all part of the attributes that made Crosby a national institution.

His golf matches with Hope during WWII were not only good for a million laughs as the ad-libs far outshone the hooks and the slices, but they always raised thousands of dollars for charities. It was their habit after the match to auction off their golf clubs and togs to buyers of war bonds. What Bing should have done was auction off his score, which was always in the 70s, to some of the duffers. They would have paid a mil' just to get into that low handicap bracket.

Bing always invested well, so between the frozen orange juice, the real estate, oil wells, owning cattle ranches and TV stations he didn't exactly have to ride around in a used car. His fun time was always when he held the Crosby Clambake, a Pro-Am golf tournament at Pebble Beach, California. More commitments were broken by big names just so they could make the opening tee-off for this match. The golfers were safe from the Highway Patrol, who thankfully weren't making drunk driving arrests as the players zigzagged those golf carts around the course. It wasn't a case of winning the trophy for the best game; it was a question of whoever was sober enough to accept the award! Crosby loved most sports and at one time owned 15 percent of the Pittsburgh Pirates and later, about 5 percent of the Detroit Tigers.

When he emerged from semi-retirement to mark 50 years in show business, he went back to his favorite vocation—raising money for charities. He did concerts at the Los Angeles Music Center, the Palladium in London and various theaters throughout Ireland and Scotland.

Hope and Crosby tee off in 1947.

He was, without a doubt, the only great entertainer who was literally knocked off his feet by a standing ovation. It was while doing a TV special at a concert in Pasadena. He was so overwhelmed by the audience's response that he tried to take one bow too many, lost his footing and fell 20 feet into the orchestra pit. This unscheduled pit stop cost him a ruptured disc and a lot of pain and suffering in the hospital. But you can't keep a good man down, and as soon as he was released, he completed his concert tour of Britain.

One unexpected aspect to this quiet and relaxed man was his quickness in responding with witty repartee to friends' taunts. Bing, onscreen and off, could easily cope with barbs from the likes of Hope, W.C. Fields, Carole Lombard or Barry Fitzgerald. He had a quality we need for a long, happy and contented life—a sense of humor. I'm sure that 14 years of doing *Road* pictures with Bob Hope helped develop that sense of humor to no end.

Bing died in one of his favorite places, on a golf course. He collapsed after finishing a round at the La Moraleja Club outside of Madrid, Spain. The name and memory of Bing Crosby will be among us for many generations to come—and rightfully so. He was one of the good guys.

JOHN WAYNE

Down through the years we've all known someone who was a name-dropper. But the real inventors of name-dropping were the motion picture studios. For the sake of publicity or advertising they made probably 95 percent of the performers drop the name they were born with and change their handle to something easier to remember. Arnold Schwarzenegger must have really flexed his muscles and fought like a bull steer when they probably tried to change his name to Arn Schwartz, to make it a shorty. I always thought the only ones who tried several names were members of the criminal element who came up with all kinds of different monikers to help keep them out of the pokey.

One of the victims of the name-dropping game was John Wayne—but only for a short while. John, whose birth name was Marion Morrison, made the jump from the Southern California University football team huddle to the Hollywood muddle. He labored on the Fox lot as a studio prop man until he got a break in small roles that ended up in a name change to Duke Morrison. After he was really discovered, it went back to John Wayne, where he became the KING and one of the busiest of Hollywood's leading men. With lead roles in such biggies as *The Quiet Man*, *The Big Trail*, *Stagecoach* and *The Searchers*, his popularity finally won him an Oscar for *True Grit* but which he really deserved for *The Quiet Man*. I had true grit while doing a caricature of the Duke, who if he didn't like it could have stuffed me in his oversized cowboy hat!

GROUCHO MARX

To waitress: "Have you got any stewed prunes?"

Waitress: "Yes."

To waitress: "Well, give 'em some black coffee. That'll sober 'em up."

Who else but Groucho Marx could have pulled a gag like that without getting shot at dawn? But if you didn't like that one, Groucho always had a million one-liners waiting in the wings. Although Groucho was a self-educated man, he didn't start out as one would suspect, just reading *College Humor*. As a kid, he had been a real bookworm. The only thing he didn't learn from the books was how to hide his money so the crafty landladies wouldn't lay their meathooks on it. He almost gave up his young career in show business because every time he went out on the road, he got stranded.

Trying to follow in the footsteps of his uncle Al Shean, who had been very successful in vaudeville, Groucho, at age 15, answered an ad for a boy singer, an ad that ran in the classifieds in a New York paper. This was hardly the way most entered the entertainment world…through classifieds! What was at the other end of the ad showed him that you should only turn to the classifieds to buy a used car. The person who had run the ad, who seemed a "nice fellow," greeted him at the door. As long as it was a job, Groucho couldn't care less, so he went on tour with this "nice fellow" and one of his friends. The tour turned out to be very short when Groucho's two companions decided to elope. Marx had earned enough money to get himself back home, but like any young guy who trusts everybody in the world, he had stuffed the money inside his pillow. To any sharp cleaning landlady, "pillow" is the secret word when they're looking for loose money to spend down at the bingo parlor.

His next try was with Gus Edwards' show *Boys and Girls*, but when the show went on tour, Marx decided to join a dramatic troupe. He was in a groove because this show lasted eight weeks before it folded, and Groucho was stranded again, and by the same culprit, an elopement. The leading lady took off with an animal trainer in the show, and when Groucho went back to the boarding house to retrieve his money for the ticket back home, the landlady had "retrieved" it before him. After that second horrifying experience, I'm sure he spent the rest of his born days trying to find a place to hide his

money. His job was with a traveling musical show, which was a nice way of disguising its actual title, which was burlesque. After trying and trying again but mostly unsuccessfully, he decided to join up with his brothers. By this time he had begun smoking cigars, which became his trademark. Later in life, a cigar maker's organization said he was the most famous cigar smoker in the world. Winston Churchill thought it was a bum selection.

The boys were a little screwed up as to their heritage—in the act at least, Groucho played the role of a German schoolteacher, Harpo played a character named Patsy Brannigan and Chico was running around looking like the little ol' Italian winemaker. With the beginning of WWI, there was such an anti-German sentiment that Groucho dropped his German character in favor of a Jewish schoolteacher.

Groucho is another of the stars with a nickname for a first name and he, like Bing Crosby, picked his up from a comic strip. *Sherlocko—the Monk,* later to become known as *Hawkshaw—the Detective,* was the source of the name. The little guy in the strip was called "Groucho" and he had a sharp, critical tongue that fit Julius (now Groucho) Marx's moody personality.

The Marx Brothers worked very hard at their chosen profession. At the beginning, they were not the roaring success they would prove to be later, but they were learning the trade by the motto "If you're not funny the first time, try, try, again." They worked well together because they didn't attempt to top each other…they each tried to get their own laughs in the way they did their part in the skit. Four shows a day and five on weekends was vaudeville's apprenticeship, and the trick was to play as many theaters in as many towns as you could until you had perfected your act. To get a laugh at the same spot in your routine every time was an art, and timing was the key.

Their years in vaudeville were all the basic training the Marx Brothers needed to hone their craft and gain fame first on Broadway, then in Hollywood in motion pictures, and finally for Groucho himself, on radio and television. Most of their movies seemed as though they were writing or adlibbing the script as it was shot, but to this day they are still film lovers' favorites.

One of their most popular movies now and in 1935 when it was made was *A Night at the Opera*, which was produced by Irving Thalberg for MGM. Irving was a very conservative, business-type man, who was only interested in the end result. When he signed the contract with the Marx Brothers, he didn't realize he had just opened the door to the nuthouse. On one occasion, Irving, a very busy entrepreneur, had an appointment at his office with the Marxes. They were on time, but Irving got into one of his hang-ups and didn't show up for two hours. This "sorry I got delayed" routine of Thalberg's had happened to the boys several times before, so they decided to do something about it.

When Irving finally arrived, he found Groucho, Harpo and Chico huddled in front of his fireplace, with a roaring fire going, roasting potatoes, and completely nude. Thalberg had just been initiated into a bit of Marx Brothers madness. Another chapter was written when Groucho was out playing golf one day. He was a lousy golfer at best and this particular course overlooking the Pacific Ocean was just too much for him to handle, so he walked to the precipice overlooking the ocean, dropped the golf balls into the water one by one, then tossed his golf bag full of expensive clubs in after them. It was a typical Groucho stunt, but he had actually followed through on something every golfer has threatened.

Harpo and Groucho Marx in *Horsefeathers*

In 1947, Groucho had the chance to do the quiz show *You Bet Your Life* on ABC, and when the show hit the number-six spot in the ratings, it moved to CBS. Just before proceeding on and moving to NBC television, Groucho made his last film with his brothers, *Love Happy*. What turned out to be the most outstanding result of the film was the hiring of a very sexy-looking blonde gal to do a bit with Groucho. The girl's name was Marilyn Monroe. He said, "I have no advice to give young actors—to young struggling actresses, my advice is to keep struggling. If you struggle long enough, you'll never get in trouble and if you never get in trouble, you will never be much of an actress." Unquote!

HARPO MARX

One of the funniest comedians of our times got his laughs without even opening his mouth. You think that was easy? But by looks and pantomime, Harpo Marx got the chuckles the other brothers had missed.

Harpo had his problems early on in life. He gave up school in second grade because the tougher guys in the class used him as a football and then threw him out of a classroom window because he was Jewish. His education came from trying to stay alive on the streets of New York City. After working and losing many jobs, among them playing piano in a house of ill repute, he joined his starving brothers at the insistence of their mother Minnie. The boys had been trying to make a go of it as a singing group but realized they were on the road to oblivion, so they decided singing was for the birds and changed to a wacky comedy act. The other brothers were quicker on the adlib, so they insisted Harpo be the silent one, which didn't go over that big with Harpo. He felt if he always had to be quiet he would show them, so he put a harp in the act, which he played very well. That was probably what picked up his name, which went along just fine with the others: Groucho, Chico, Gummo and Zeppo. With appellations like that, they were bound to be a wacky comedy act. I didn't know I was drawing a "Gookie," but that's what Harpo named the character he was playing.

The Marx Brothers pose for a publicity shot for *Animal Crackers*.

BETTE DAVIS

They say imitation is the sincerest form of flattery. At that rate, Bette Davis must have been the most flattered person in the world because she was certainly the most imitated. You never saw anyone doing a take-off on Esther Williams diving into the aqua blue water or Sonja Henie, skating across a frozen pond, but everyone had their concept of Bette smoking a cigarette; actually, she didn't smoke it, she attacked it! But this is not the stuff of which a great actress is made. This was just more or less a gimmick used by a very talented lady.

As you can well imagine, Bette Davis wanted to be an actress from the time she was a little girl. However, her youthful desire almost cost her her life. She had her first acting part in a school Christmas pageant. Would you believe—Bette was Santa Claus—a thin one, but nevertheless, Santa Claus. When she struck the match to light the candles, part of the match dropped on her costume and started to burn. Her Santa Claus whiskers caught fire and Bette's face was severely burned. Fortunately for Warner Bros., although they didn't know it at the time, her face was completely healed.

Bette Davis and William Wyler during filming of *Jezebel*

She made her way through high school theatricals and into the John Murray Anderson dramatic school in New York, where she won a scholarship. It was while she was doing a show in New York that she made a screen test and was signed by Universal Studios. She said at the time she arrived in Hollywood, "I had about as much sex appeal as Slim Summerville." You wouldn't know it, but in her first shootings on the set, Bette choked at the sight of the one-eyed monster they call a camera. As a result, she would constantly turn her back on it and the studio got some of the best "over the shoulder" shots of Bette Davis ever seen. Even her shoulders didn't look that good to Universal, so they dropped her option in file 13 after several unmemorable movies including *Hell's House* in 1932.

Bette was about to flee back to New York when "that certain phone call" came through—and you thought those only happened in the movies. The caller was George Arliss and he offered her a role in *The Man Who Played God* (1932). Arliss played Him before George Burns!

It was W. Somerset Maugham's *Of Human Bondage* (1934) that really gained her recognition as an actress and the next year she won an Oscar for *Dangerous* (1935), but everyone knows the Oscar was really for *Of Human Bondage*. Bette discovered once you have an Oscar in your home, you always have relatives, so she had to "take in" another one for her role in *Jezebel* (1938). She was nominated so many times (11), they should have just put her name on the program for the Academy Awards night.

The intensity that Bette Davis put into her stage and film work carried over into any other project in which she was involved. She was the President of the Motion Picture Academy of Arts and Sciences and was the first President of the Hollywood Canteen. As if that wasn't enough, she was also President of the Tailwagger Foundation, an organization sponsoring humane legislation for animals. Bette was also active in promoting the training of guide dogs for the blind.

When you see the name Bette Davis you will never be disappointed. She was the consummate actress and played each role to the hilt. She learned her "gift of giving" from her first portrayal of Santa Claus.

RED SKELTON

At that time the Derby had a lot of good guys coming in—the place really had some romance going for it. It was always lit up like High Mass. When any celeb walked in the front door you were aware of who it was, no matter where you were sitting.

Red Skelton would arrive with the entire crew from his radio show, which was on the air across the street at the Lux Radio Theatre. As soon as he came in he would do a pratfall. Crash—and everyone knew Red was among us. Pratfalls were routine for Red. He had gone the whole route from circus clown to tent shows, and from there to showboats, burlesque, vaudeville and nightclubs. By the age of 10 he was matching his wage with his age by working in a medicine show. At 12 he was in a minstrel show and by 14 he was touring the Mississippi on the showboat *Cotton Blossom*.

Red followed in his father's (oversized) footsteps when he became a circus clown. His Dad was a famous clown with the renowned Hagenbeck & Wallace Circus. Red not only become famous himself for his clowning around, but he was also famous for the clown faces he painted on canvas. Any of the better art galleries will have a Red Skelton clown painting on display. He was proud to claim the dubious title of "one of the oldest comedians" in the business, but much before that time, he had earned the title of "youngest comedian" in vaudeville.

His doughnut dunking routine hilariously demonstrated how, in a crowded restaurant, people dunk their donuts in their coffee and his take-off of a radio announcer getting smashed while extolling the virtues of "Guzzlers Gin" were two of the funniest pieces of business ever seen on a vaudeville stage. As his paycheck grew, so did his popularity in nightclubs and theaters.

Once he hit the network radio airwaves, national recognition was Red's. Shortly thereafter, MGM beckoned and Skelton added more credits to his crowded and lustrous resume. He was rolling into high gear when the politicians decided to stage WWII and Red became just another draftee. To keep his hand in, Skelton staged shows in Army camps and hospitals here and in the Mediterranean theater. Some of his shows were so close to the front lines that Red was being shot at and not because of his material. When he got discharged, Red laughed (he always laughed) and said, "I'm the only Hollywood star to leave the service the same grade I entered—a private!" Major Clark Gable and Lieutenant Robert Taylor were just a couple of his fellow entertainers who outranked him.

When it came to comedy he is one guy you could always say was a "natural."

CHARLTON HESTON

There's one actor who has been the President of the United States so many times, he doesn't want the job the other actor really got. But he would have made some kind of a President—because for openers, he can part the Red Sea. I don't know how that would help inflation—unless he drowned it when he let the sea go back. The actor (who got an honorary degree from the Plumber's Union for the job on the Red Sea) is Charlton Heston. Charlton deserves a lot of credit—anyone who can get the role of Moses and not even have to audition for the Lord is some kind of an actor.

As I was drawing him I needled him, "How am I ever going to get that broken nose on paper?" He said, "Don't make fun of that nose. It's helped me make a good living for 30 years." The broken nose came from playing high school football—but Heston has never been bitter about it because he feels it helped him to get a lot of parts for which he might otherwise have been passed over. Football became a thing of the past when Charlton got into an excellent dramatics program at New Trier High School in Winnetka, Illinois. He admits he can't remember when he didn't want to be an actor.

Charlton Heston studio portrait

His very first role as a thespian was at the age of five. He played Santa Claus in a Christmas pageant. It's the last fat man he has ever played.

Eventually, he went to Northwestern University in Evanston, Illinois on an acting scholarship. He did a little moonlighting during his education by appearing on radio shows in Chicago. Everything took a backseat while Charlton served with the Army Air Forces in the Aleutians in WWII. After he returned, he made a couple of forays to New York before he landed a part in the Catherine Cornell production of *An-*

CHARLTON HESTON

Charlton Heston checks out his caricature that I have just finished.

thony and Cleopatra. After several years trodding the boards on Broadway, television came into its own and Charlton practically made a home out of Studio One. His performances were noticed by the right people—one of them Hal B. Wallis, who was an independent producer at Paramount Pictures. Hal was so impressed he signed Heston to a contract without even making him go through the ritual of a screen test.

Since his debut in his first movie *Peer Gynt* (1941), he has acted in better than 82 pictures—the whole range from Biblical to disaster, science fiction to horror films, plus played three different Presidents onscreen.

He loved his career as a professional actor and when another movie wasn't in the immediate offing, he headed for a stage production.

Heston had an arrangement with the Ahmanson Theatre in Los Angeles to perform in a play every other year. Being in as much demand as he was in the motion picture business, he had neither the time nor the desire for touring theatrical companies, which he feels may be a thing of the past. With the tremendous cost and complexity of staging a show in different theaters that are not equipped to cope with the demands of a traveling company, he feels future productions will have to emanate from the eight major cities where theaters thrive.

As much as Charlton appreciates the legitimate theater he can still thank the movie industry for earning him awards in 20 different countries. And he can always be grateful to Cecil B. DeMille for selecting him to play the role of Moses in the Oscar-winning *The Ten Commandments*. DeMille chose Heston not only because he was an excellent actor but also because he bore a marked resemblance to Michelangelo's statue "Moses in the Temple" —including the broken nose. So you gotta say one thing—Charlton Heston's got a nose for business.

Charlton Heston in *Planet of the Apes*

JUDY GARLAND

In spite of being born with the name Frances Gumm, she became a legend in our time and for years to come, and that was the immortal Judy Garland. I was witness to her effect on film audiences while attending one of her very first film appearances. It was in 1936 when I was in show biz while working a theater in Denver. I went to see a movie and it was the first time I ever heard a movie theater audience applauding like mad. The reason was to honor a very young girl in *Pigskin Parade*. She sang one song and the moviegoers loved it and reacted as though she were on the stage. The little vocalist was of course Judy. From that great performance she really reached stardom when she played and sang in *The Wizard of Oz*. She actually went "Over the Rainbow" when the Academy awarded her a special Juvenile Oscar for her outstanding juvenile performances in 1940. She became a part of the Hardy Family in several films she did with Mickey Rooney playing Betsy Booth.

Unfortunately, to keep her on the road to success, the studio put her on sleeping pills and barbiturates to keep her "up," but all they did was "down" the rest of her life. She knew she needed help, so she tried to find a man who could do just that for her, but after four tries, she knew that wasn't going to be her answer. One of them, Sid Luft, did produce *A Star Is Born*, which many critics felt was Judy's best-ever performance on the screen. She received an Academy Award nomination and was considered a shoo-in, but Joan Crawford beat her out for *Mildred Pierce*. Judy was in the hospital at the time because of the birth of her son Joey and had been prepped to accept her Oscar live from her hospital bed. She was crushed to lose the coveted award.

Judy from *A Star Is Born*

Judy spent the rest of her life listening to and enjoying the thrill of tremendous applause with many standing ovations from her concert performances. She proved to be one of the most famous entertainers in Hollywood history. Minnesota will never forget her—they have established a Judy Garland Museum, and we will never forget her as we view and love her in the many, many reruns on TV of *The Wizard of Oz*.

JOHNNY CARSON

There were two people whose caricatures the Derby wanted on their wall but I had to draw them someplace else—and with good reason. Each time one of them got out there among crowds they were mobbed by the public. One was Burt Reynolds and the other was Johnny Carson. In Burt's case I had to go to Paramount Studios to draw him on the set, and even there he had people yakking at him so they could say they had talked to Burt Reynolds. Carson sat for me in his office at NBC and when I finished the drawing, his secretary came in and told him his next appointment had arrived and brought five people with him. Johnny almost had a coronary. Here he had a business appointment with one guy and he brings all of his relatives to meet Carson. Which just goes to show that once you're a celebrity, you don't own yourself, the public owns you.

Corning, Iowa is a long distance from New York City but Johnny Carson made the trip in giant strides. Starting out as a comedy writer for radio shows, Johnny moved on to hosting an afternoon TV show in L.A. Next stop was New York and he timed it perfectly, because he took over as host of the *Tonight Show* and made a career of it. He became a superstar, setting records for doing over 6,500 shows, interviewing more than 20,000 guests, most of them the top celebs of all times, and put out 700,000 gags without once using a laugh track. I held up my caricature and said, "Heeerree's Johnny"... and Carson said, "Johnny who?" I didn't laugh.

CARY GRANT

Here's a question for you, was the *reel* name his *real* name? I'll save you the trouble of guessing. Nope! His real name was Archibald Leach but his reel name, the name he is known and adored by, was Cary Grant. He was always impeccably dressed, always a gentleman. In the 75 movies he appeared in, none would be classified as a sordid film. The only four-letter word used in any of them was L-O-V-E. He was a master of all genres including mysteries and suspense such as *North by Northwest* (1959) and *Indiscreet* (1958), dramas like *Penny Serenade* (1941) and a myriad of brilliant comedies that include *Bringing Up Baby* (1938), *My Favorite Wife* (1940) and *The Philadelphia Story* (1940). Some of his movies supported the WWII war effort, such as the film short *The Road to Victory* in 1944.

Cary wrote these words of wisdom in his autobiography: "So many of us think that the acquisition of money can bring self-esteem and happiness. Money attracts more envy than empathy...more lust than love." These are indeed thoughts from which we can benefit.

And I would add one more thing that money can't buy...good health!

Cary lived in Hollywood for more than 30 years and I'll guarantee you he was never once evicted for nonpayment of rent.

CLARK GABLE

As far as fan clubs were concerned, Clark Gable had them locked in long before *It Happened One Night*. He was Hollywood's "Big Man," one of the film colony's most highly respected actors. His greatest attribute was that he wasn't a put-on—a phony. His logic about the business was strictly down to earth. He knew that the public loved the big stars, made a fuss over them and idolized their every move.

But in the long run, in Tinsel Town you could go from distinction to extinction in a heartbeat. Gable was fondly known as "King" but he was well aware of the fact that you were only "King" as long as that guy out there kept buying tickets to see your films. The "hatchet man" was always waiting in the wings ready to cut your props out from under you at the first sign of weakening audience appeal.

To Gable, Hollywood was a place to make your money, enjoy it while it was there, and then forget the whole thing. He had been exposed to it all and knew the executives could make you, break you, and then toss you out for the next rubbish collection. His attitude was take me or leave me, who needs you. Some of that must have carried over into his marital efforts because although he tried it five times, it never seemed to work out. It was while he was going through the motions of one of his marriages that he met Carole Lombard. Carole proved to be one of Gable's "kind of folks." She was a wild one—uninhibited. She appealed to Clark because of her desire to keep her private life private. That even included dining at the Hollywood Brown Derby, which they did quite often. They would seldom sit in the main dining room but usually were ushered back to the pri-

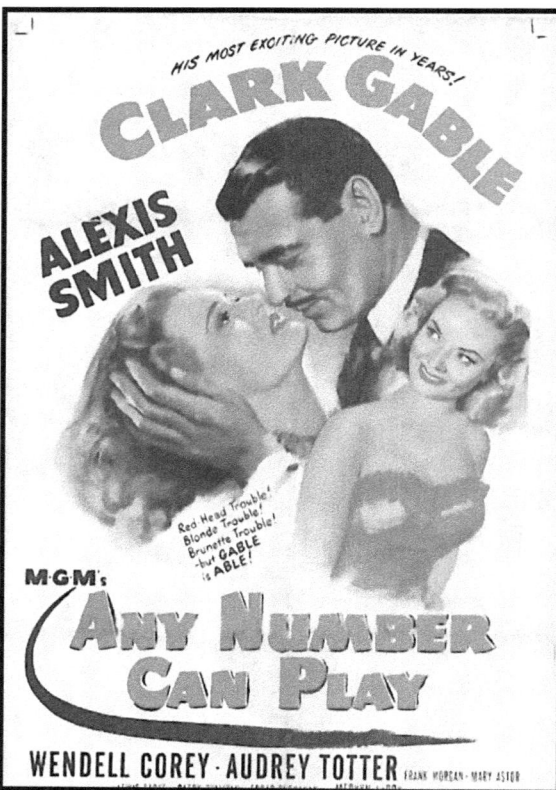

Carole Lombard and Clark Gable

vacy of the American Room. It wasn't a case of being aloof; they just wanted to be alone. Gable adored Carole because she could out-hunt him, out-fish him, and out-drink him, which was no mean feat.

The two of them were in the first stages of being roommates but their careers got in the way. The studio bosses got into the act and put a kibosh on the whole thing because of the threatened box office boycott by church groups and moral organizations. Carole and Clark married in 1939 much to the relief of everyone. They led a happy but tumultuous life until January 16, 1942. Carole had been making personal appearances on behalf of the first war bond drive of WWII. Her mother accompanied her on the trip and the two of them dined at the Hollywood Brown Derby the night of their initial departure. She told Benny, their favorite waiter, "Take good care of Pappy for me." On their scheduled return from the tour, Carole was so anxious to get back to Clark that she had to use every wile at her disposal to get on that plane. Civilians, no matter who they were, just didn't take plane seats away from military personnel. Carole wrangled as only she could, and finally, along with her mother, boarded that fatal flight. The plane crashed just 48 feet from the top of a Vegas mountain. Eyewitnesses said there was not one piece of the plane left that measured 10 feet in length. Gable was beside himself with grief and turned into a recluse. The studio enticed him out of his loner role to do one movie, but then he quietly enlisted in the Army Air Corps and went to Florida for Officer training. It was tougher on Gable than it would have been on your average guy. His fellow trainees looked upon him either as a real nice guy or as a "showboat" because here was this big star who had volunteered to get into this thing.

He received his commission as a lieutenant and won his wings as a gunner. Gable put his knowledge of what it takes to get a film made to work and formed a photographic unit that was sent to England. He was really doing a wonderful job and was soon promoted to captain. In addition, he proved to all he wasn't a movie malingerer when he earned the Air Medal for "Exceptionally Meritorious Achievement" in five bomber combat missions.

In 1943 he was returned to the U.S. and assigned the task of editing the motion pictures taken during forays over Europe for the First Motion Picture Unit. These films were then used for training purposes. It was while he was in Washington showing the films to the Army Air Chiefs, that Captain Gable became Major Gable in recognition of his further services to the Air Corps.

After Gable finally put his uniform back in the closet he returned to Metro-Goldwyn-Mayer to make a series of successful pictures: *Adventure* (1945) with Greer Garson, *The Hucksters* (1947) with Deborah Kerr and *Homecoming* (1948) with Lana Turner, Anne Baxter and John Hodiak. He hadn't lost his old box office appeal! But all was not going well because Gable was not a happy man. He was not satisfied with the quality of the pictures being offered to him. His fans had always looked on him as a two-fisted, red-blooded he-man, who knew how to kiss a woman so it didn't look as though she was being swallowed alive. Unlike today's would-be screen lovers he knew how to deliver a kiss. However, the gray began to make itself known in the hair and the chest began to ease into the waistline. Hollywood began to offer him more mature roles. Clark turned to his Scotch bottle for consolation. It didn't make him feel any younger but it sure put a nice, hazy glow around the facts of life.

Gable had many close calls in making his pictures but the one that fractured all concerned was in the filming of the earthquake scene in *San Francisco*. A prop wall of wooden bricks fell on him and frantic extras and crew hands dug him out while paramedics gave mouth-to-mouth

Clark Gable in 1934

81

Hedda Hopper and Clark Gable share a laugh on a radio program in 1950.

resuscitation to revive the frantic producer and the director. The accident caused no damage and failed to pin his ears back, which were a conversation piece all of his movie life. In his first big picture Irving Thalberg described him as having "ears like a bat."

Typical of the bizarre things that can only happen in Hollywood, Gable did *not* win an Oscar for *Gone With the Wind*. It was always a financial whammer at the box office and to this day, *Gone With the Wind* attracts a bigger audience on TV than the World Series. In 1939 Clark said *goodbye* to the Oscar that went to Robert Donat for his performance in *Goodbye, Mr. Chips*. Poor Margaret Mitchell, the authoress of *GWTW*, who had almost killed herself over the horrendous task of completing her novel, died penniless after being struck down by an automobile in her hometown of Atlanta, Georgia.

As with most of the big stars of his era, Gable paid his dues in radio. In the '30s and '40s, radio really came into its own with all the talent available to the networks. With 40 to 50 million people listening to the *Lux Radio Theatre*, the booming personalities could ill afford to miss out on this kind of exposure. Two other shows that drew big audiences were Louella Parsons' *Hollywood Hotel* and *Hedda Hopper's Hollywood*. To the stars' dismay they were practically forced to appear on these two shows for no salary; they were pretty much blackmailed into doing them just to avoid adverse publicity and poor reviews from the girls.

Clark Gable and Claudette Colbert in *It Happened One Night*

However, what most stars did enjoy was being on the Bing Crosby, Bob Hope, Jack Benny and Edgar Bergen shows because of the great scripts and their excellent following. Even F.D.R. saw the advantages of radio and used it to get his ideas out to the people. His Fireside Chats set an example for all following Presidents, but to do their radio thing they forsook the coziness of burning logs for a comfy chair in the Oval Office.

As they did in the early days of the talkies, the motion picture industry began to see the benefits of stealing radio talent: Kate Smith, Ed Wynn, Burns and Allen, Jack Benny, Rudy Vallee, Edgar Bergen and his motley friends, Benny Goodman, Tommy Dorsey, Red Skelton, Arthur Godfrey and Frank Sinatra made the big jump from radio to movies with varying degrees of success. Radio was certainly responsible for the Big Band craze. The millions of listeners, who did the glide and the dip on their kitchen floor while listening to a Guy Lombardo, Wayne King, or Glen Miller broadcast, would flock to the ballrooms and nightclubs to see their favorite bandleaders live. Then they would do a repeat performance when their musical maestros would appear in a movie. Some of their heroes couldn't talk too good—but what the heck, the music was fantastic. Look what radio and later TV did for Guy Lombardo. How many romantic New Year's Eves began by listening to Guy Lombardo and his Royal Canadians, who helped millions welcome in the New Year?

CAROL BURNETT

Being versatile means "being competent in many things," but if you're looking for the true meaning of versatile, all you have to do is see Carol Burnett in anything. And one of the things she does best is collect Emmys. She ain't bad on the silver screen either.

Carol has all the attributes of the natural comedienne—the timing, the clowning, the slapstick and the out and out buffoonery. To top it all off, she has the voice to sing everything from a popular ballad to an operatic aria while suffering from the hiccups. She knew what she wanted to do in life the first time she discovered that when you kick up your heels in fun, people laugh. It really started at a time when she was majoring in journalism at the University of California in Los Angeles. She was studying playwriting and part of the curriculum was to perform onstage. That did it! Once she heard laughter she knew that was her kind of music. She joined an opera workshop at school and that really paid off for her. At a private party Carol teamed with a young man in the group to do scenes from *Annie Get Your Gun*. One of the guests was so impressed with their talent he staked them to a loan of $1,000

each to get a start in show business. He had a couple of stipulations in the deal, but they were pleasant. All he wanted them to do was head for New York and try to get their careers under way. He gave them five years to return the loan to him. In due time all the conditions were met.

Carol bowed out of college and made tracks for New York. Aspiring actresses like herself had a haven there, the famous Rehearsal Club. Of course, there was a stipend for room and board, and since very few had a stage gig when they first arrive, she had to get a part-time job. Luckily she

Harvey Korman and Carol Burnett in their infamous *Sunset Blvd.* takeoff

had a semi-college education because it got her a position as a hatcheck girl in a restaurant in Rockefeller Center. (You've got to be smart to know a 6 7/8 hat from a 7 1/4.) The job left her plenty of time to see theatrical agents but they didn't have any time to see her. It was the same old chestnut, "We can't get you a booking until we see your work, so have somebody else get you something and we'll come and catch your act." They weren't going to stymie Carol Burnett that way. As President of the Rehearsal Club (an office she had been elected to by the other gals) she got everyone to chip in so they could hire a rehearsal hall and invite all the agents in the city to come and see them perform. It worked for her—she acquired a well-known Broadway agent. After a few nondescript jobs she got her first television break on the Paul

Jack Lemmon, Carol Burnett and Walter Matthew in *The Front Page*

Winchell show, *The Speidel Show*, as the girlfriend to Winchell's dummies. All she did was sing on the show so she didn't have to sit on Paul's lap with his other friends.

In 1956 she appeared on a Garry Moore morning show on CBS and it was "instant success." From there on all the doors were open.

She did a number at the Blue Angel nightclub in New York entitled, "I Made a Fool of Myself Over John Foster Dulles"—even Secretary of State Dulles obligingly helped her career. The song did nothing for Dulles but it put Carol on the Jack Parr *Tonight Show* (1957) and got her several appearances on the Ed Sullivan program *Toast of the Town* (1957-1958).

Meanwhile, back at *The Garry Moore Show*, they were waiting for Carol with a contract and it became her training ground for future Carol Burnett shows. Her flair for playing oddball females became a part of her perennial retinue of characters. Her impersonations of the "distaff side of the theater" are caricatures come to life. Carol has made a career of being a very funny lady, but some of the serious roles she has handled on the big screen and TV show that the time she spent in the University of California theater arts department paid off. She also proved that jocks aren't the only ones who go to college and come out and make big money!

ROY ROGERS

Most parents will tell you that Santa Claus is a shy old guy, but did you know that on one occasion, Santa Claus' real name was Slye? Leonard Slye, that is. Of course most folks would know that particular Santa Claus better by his legally adopted name of Roy Rogers. Leonard…or Roy…or Santa…or whoever he was, had his first dramatic role in grammar school, playing St. Nick in a school play. He hadn't gone Western yet, so Santa didn't come in on a horse, twanging a guitar.

Roy's ambition was to be a dentist, but once he learned to sing hillbilly and Western songs, it was like pulling teeth to get him to stay in high school. It took one family visit to California to convince Rogers that living in his hometown of Duck Run, Ohio, was for the birds. He took a slow, short-term job for a paycheck, rode back to Los Angeles and formed a cowboy band to appear on a radio amateur contest. If Hollywood was writing his script, he would have won the contest, but he didn't. Roy knew you can't win 'em all, so he kept plugging away and later formed the group he was associated with for years, Sons of the Pioneers. After the usual "brainstorming," they settled down to singing on an L.A. station and making recordings of their hillbilly

Dale Evans and Roy Rogers

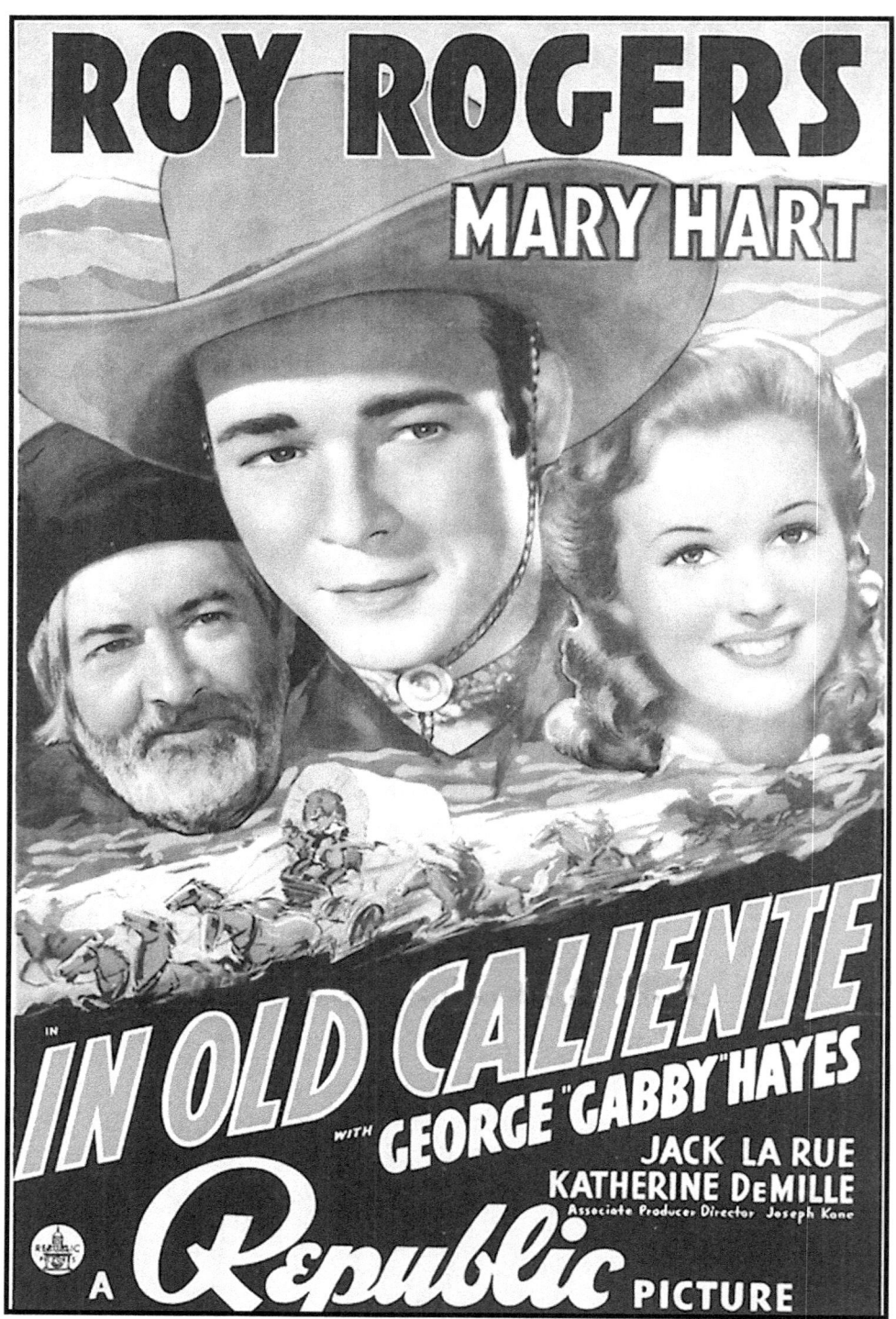

songs. "The Last Roundup" was the record that turned out to be "the first opportunity" for Roy and the boys as, they were given some hit parts in Republic Pictures Western films. One of those pictures was *The Big Show* (1936) and it made Gene Autry Hollywood's most popular cowboy film star. What Gene didn't know was that his closest contender for his title was accompanying him in the background with the Sons of the Pioneers.

Roy's initial starring role came about because he was good at eavesdropping and fleet of foot. He was in a hat shop when a guy rushed in, dressed in typical movie cowboy outfit, and pleaded for a 10-gallon hat because Republic Studios was holding screen tests looking for the "right" Western personality. Roy made the studio gate in nothing flat, got the test and the leading role in *Under Western Stars* (1938).

Roy Rogers in 1940

Most of Roy's subsequent pictures, all excellent box office earners, consisted of "a little singing, a little riding, a little shooting and a girl who had to be saved in the nick of time." And of course, the girl always got second billing to Roy's horse, Trigger. The colt could perform 50 tricks, which was just 49 more than the girl could. The beauty of making Westerns was that Roy never had to assume a role—he just played himself, Roy Rogers. That was good enough to place him first among Western stars in 1948 and earned him the distinction of the "world's top boots-and-saddle star." This was because he outranked all other cowboy stars at the Taj Mahal of the theatrical world, the box office. Roy and Trigger left their boot and hoof prints in the wet concrete…not outside of Grauman's Chinese Theatre, but a theater called The Hitching Post. It derived its name from the fact that it had a genuine hitching post just outside its box office. With all the money he earned from rodeo appearances, his radio programs, his movies and his recordings of old and new Western songs, Roy proved that all successful cowboys don't necessarily have to come from Texas. There was one gun-totin', high-ridin' moneymaker who came out of Duck Run, Ohio.

JACK PAAR

The night I drew Jack Paar at the Derby he was so shook up that even his bow tie was quivering. He had just completed a highly successful summer on radio as Jack Benny's replacement, was selected in a magazine poll as the Most Promising Star of Tomorrow, held the listening audience in the palm of his hand, and the network has just handed him one of their typical *bon voyages*—"Thank you…but don't call us, we'll call you."

Jack was sitting in the booth with friends and the more I drew, the sadder he got. Not at me, because nobody ever gets a look see at my masterpiece until I am finished and just in case, I have one foot braced under the chair for a quick dash to the exit. No, he just could not see how they would possibly give him that kind of a brush off when he had done so well. He informed his friends that he had had it with Hollywood and was heading for New York, where even if you get mugged, the muggers were more sympathetic than Hollywood producers. The people standing by watching the mugging won't help you but at least they'll feel sorry for you. Even New York wasn't ready to give Jack the key to the city, so he had to wade through one radio or television show after the other. In 1952, he got a television show of his own, *Up to Paar* but his audience was a no show. He took on the *CBS-TV Morning Show* in 1954 but this time the sponsors were a no show. He tried an afternoon CBS-TV show and an ABC radio program but both defaulted.

It wasn't until he was given the NBC-TV *Tonight Show* that things started popping for Paar. This was exactly 10 years after I had done his caricature and witnessed his depressed tirade about Hollywood's idiosyncrasies. It just proved that Paar had perseverance.

When Jack made his debut they were up to 38 sponsors. Of course *The Tonight Show* (which for some reason or other was later remembered as The Johnny Carson Show) now has so many sponsors, they interrupt the commercials on occasion and sneak in a guest star. The success of the show in getting people off the sleeping pill and turned on to late night TV was attributed to Jack's impromptu informality and his wise selection of guest performers. Paar often let a little frigid sarcasm sneak into his humor, but this could be attributed to the fact that in order to help cure his teenage tuberculosis, he had worked with a railroad gang in freezing weather—he just hadn't thawed out yet. As a kid he also stuttered and in order to cure himself, he would put a button in his mouth and read aloud. It was when he swallowed the upper and lower button of his pants and he had to pull the belt tighter to hold them up that he cured his stuttering. *Radio-TV Daily* named Jack the "Man of the

Year" in television for 1957 and 1958 and *The Tonight Show* was selected as the outstanding comedy series. With that feather in his cap, NBC changed the program's name to *The Jack Paar Show*, which remained the title until Jack left the show.

Paar always said, "I like to think of myself not as a comic but as a humorist. To me, a comic says funny things. A humorist thinks funny things." As you can see by his expression on my caricature, he must have been thinking of something funny, even though he was as mad as a wet hen.

JASCHA HEIFETZ

I'm not a pediatrician, but how would it grab you if I told you every time your child cries, play music for him or her? Believe me when I tell you, it could pay off. It did in the case of Jascha Heifetz. He stopped crying and loved music so much he went on to become one of the world's most famous violinist. His parents were so happy to discover the secret of how to end his flow of tears using music that they purchased a quarter-sized violin for Jascha. He began his lessons at the age of three. This is when most kids are learning to wave bye-bye. Heifetz must have been slow in adapting himself to the instrument, because he was all the way up to the advanced age of seven before he played his first solo at the Mendelssohn Concerto at Korno, Russia. He made many public appearances in Russia and became the Burt Reynolds of the violin. Every place he played, the enthusiastic crowds would mob him and he had to have a police escort all the way home.

Child prodigies usually do an "el foldo" before they are old enough to smoke, but Jascha proved the exception. At age 17, he made his first appearance in New York at Carnegie Hall (1917), and the only ones who were nervous were the audience, which was made up of virtuosos and hypercritical skeptics. Heifetz walked onstage, deliberately tuned up his violin and started to play. The real music to his ears was the deafening applause he heard before he had completed his first selection.

He has given concerts in almost every country in the world, and he believed that the amount of traveling he did would be the equivalent of two round trips to the moon. Not only were his concerts exciting, but he always seemed to manage to land in a country just as it was about to destroy itself. He played Russia during the revolution, Japan when an earthquake hit, India while the anti-British riots were going on and Ireland at the height of the Sinn Fein uprisings. Then he really got into the thick of things by doing 45 concerts in eight weeks at army bases located near the front lines in WWII. He proved to the G.I.s that there was more to the arts than comic books and boogie-woogie. He played a Bach prelude for them. However,

Jascha Heifetz in 1937

he prefaced his performance by telling them, "This number is like spinach. You may not like it but it's good for you." He knew he had made his point when he finished and was overwhelmed by cries of "more spinach."

ALAN LADD

Universal picked Alan Ladd up with a group of college boys who were to be groomed for stardom—unfortunately his grooming "didn't take," so he was dropped after six months. Then it became "scramble time" as he took a job at Warner Bros. as a grip. He worked on a newspaper and owned and operated a hot dog stand. There were so many "hot dogs" running around Warner's at the time that his wares didn't have any appeal. He helped pad the kitty with some extra's jobs and a few readings onstage and in radio.

Sue Ladd, a former actress, was also his personal manager. When she first met Alan, she felt he had that something that makes for the big time. She got him some small parts at Republic and Monogram Studios and some lines in *Citizen Kane* and Walt Disney's *Reluctant Dragon*. His big chance came in 1942 in RKO's *Joan of Paris*. After that Paramount really started his star spinning when they cast him as the hired killer in *This Gun for Hire*. He went on to make over 90 pictures and although no one could ever accuse him of being an actor, he was still as popular as anyone who ever hit the big screen. For a guy who was only five feet, six inches tall, he became a giant in the motion picture industry.

Alan Ladd was still on top in Hollywood when I drew him. I assumed Position A, the attack position in my caricature action, drew a bead with my piercing blue eyes, and prepared to celebrate the launching of Ladd on my drawing paper. But alas! There he sat with no makeup, no fancy lights, no sneaky camera angles, and I detected not one chin—but two. Oh, the second one wasn't full-fledged yet, but it was a half a grapefruit in the making. It was obvious he had forgotten to wear his chinstrap the night before. With fiendish glee, I etched it on the paper like a guy who had just discovered champagne in his Santa Fe Wine bottle. Proud of my revealing revelation, I held my caricature up high for all to see, and Sue came unglued. How could I possibly put that soon-to-be-heir to the first chin on my drawing? The more I tried to argue with her that Alan had put that there, not me—I was just recording it for posterity—the angrier she became. Alan sat there and couldn't have cared less. He had had the fun of acquiring that thing that everyone ends up with no matter how hard they try to avoid it. Ladd was content with the thought that at least he didn't have it when he first started in 1933.

Sue's reaction to Alan's caricature just proves what I always said: "It pays to never show a wife a husband's caricature!" Here she's been living with her dreamboat all these years and she looks at my drawing and she gets all shook up about it. When I work a convention, the wife will always stand

behind me and say: "Oh, that isn't George's nose," and "George's chin doesn't stick out like that." But when I do the wife, the husband stands behind me and whispers in my ear, "Give it to her—give it to her!" Now *that* denotes typical loving marriage loyalty.

OZZIE AND HARRIET NELSON

Two of the nicest celebrities who ever walked in the Derby were Ozzie and Harriet Nelson. They never felt they were above having a warm, friendly greeting or a long conversation with you. These were the same down-to-earth folks you always saw on *The Adventures of Ozzie and Harriet*. The scripts for the show, written primarily by Ozzie, were really about the everyday happenings in the lives of the Nelson family. And there had been plenty of happenings in Ozzie's life. He was off to a miserable start when his mother named him Oswald, but before he could even learn to spell it, Oswald had been shortened to Ozzie. Everyone *except* his mother called him that. His dad, although a banker by profession, was big on putting on amateur theatricals and what could be better than to have "my son, my son" perform in them.

Ozzie would join forces with his older brother Alfred and they would sing duets in the show. They reached an artistic peak when they sang before King Albert and Cardinal Mercer in Belgium. This exciting moment came about because Ozzie had become the youngest Eagle Scout in the United States. For this reason he was invited to attend the Boy Scouts First International Jamboree, to be held in England. Brother Alfred was with the Scout delegation, which also visited France and Belgium. At every stop on their tour as well as on the bus trips along the way, the Nelson brothers entertained.

Singing wasn't Ozzie's only specialty, as he proved when he went to Rutgers University and participated in football, lacrosse, swimming, track

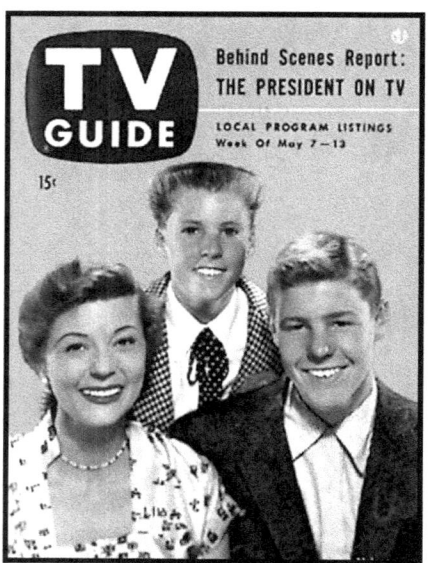

and boxing. As if that wasn't enough, he formed his own orchestra, which he fronted with his saxophone and his singing. And all the time the guy was after my job because he really wanted to be a cartoonist. You only have to have talent to play in a band, but Ozzie also had a Bachelor of Letters and a law school degree.

In 1931 Ozzie saw a Paramount short starring Rudy Vallee, *Musical Justice*, and was immediately attracted to one of the singers, Harriet Hilliard. He managed to track her down and invited her to join his band as their vocalist. At that time the Nelson Orchestra was broadcasting coast to coast from the Glen Island Casino in

New Rochelle, New York. Ozzie was lonesome singing alone, so he invited Harriet to join him in some duets, and the rest is history.

Between having sons David and Ricky, Harriet did 17 movies. Not to be outdone (although he could hardly give birth to two boys), Ozzie did seven movies, including a few they made together such as *Here Come the Nelsons* in 1952.

The Adventures of Ozzie and Harriet was a replacement for *The Red Skelton Show* when Red received word from his draft board. They moved their successful format right from radio into television and picked up a few million more Nelson lovers. The only reason you don't see Harriet Hilliard Nelson in this book is because she was such a nice person I just couldn't get my pencils to carve up this lovely lady in caricature.

JIMMY DURANTE

Bob Hope, Jimmy Durante and Fred Allen (1942)

When you talk about a famous entertainer who was great at acting, outstanding as a comedian and one of the nicest guys in show biz, and surprisingly he was a terrific ragtime piano player, the surprise is that his name was Jimmy Durante.

Durante was entranced with Dixieland jazz bands and formed a band of New Orleans musicians. Durante's Jazz and Novelty Band played at the Alamo Club in Harlem. In the 1920s he joined several eminent white jazz bands and was considered a great ragtime and jazz piano player. When we saw him on television or in the movies he always appeared a piano novice, but by this time he was a renowned comedian. He hit stardom when he appeared in a show on Broadway called *Jumbo*. By the '30s he became popular in movies and radio, and when television arrived on the scene, he moved right in. He guest starred on many popular television shows. One of his most requested songs by the public was the theme song he wrote for himself, "Inka Dinka Do."

With Jimmy there was no ego involved, but he had the quirky habit of insisting on sitting in the booth under his drawing at the Derby. If someone was already sitting there, he would come back later. He always made fun of his nose, so he wasn't about to be insulted by his caricature, even though he ended up in two frames—I was always surprised the Derby didn't charge him for that second one.

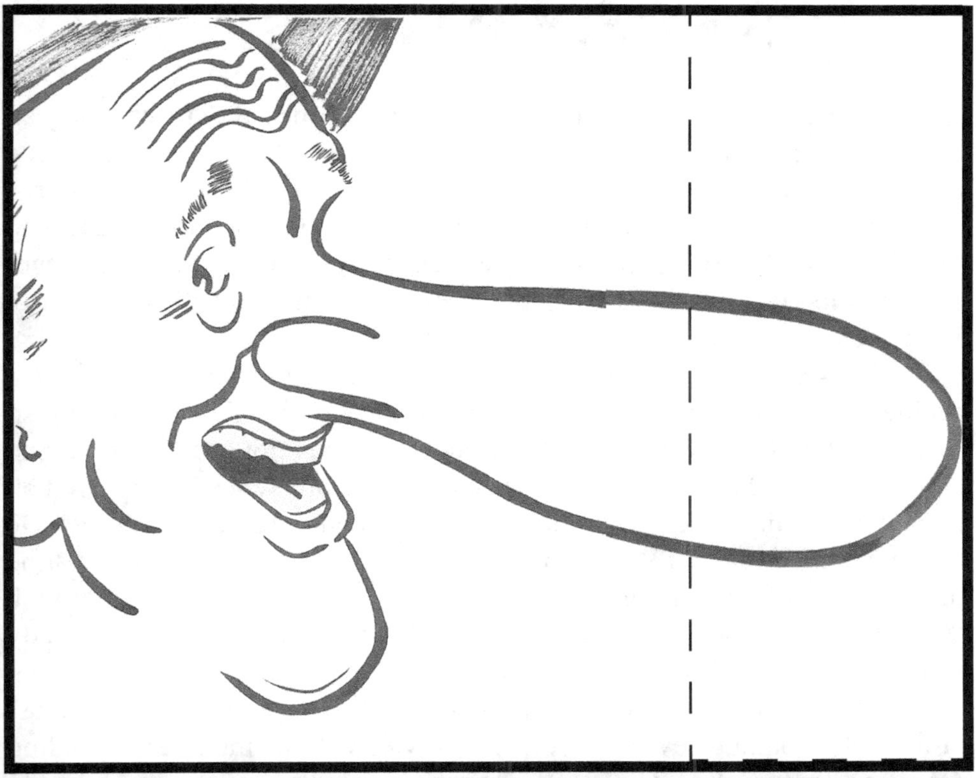

There shall be Music and Joy
Wherever he goes!
JIMMY DURANTE
THAT'S MY BOY
Set to Glorious Melody
by OSCAR STRAUS
RICHARD TAUBER · JUNE CLYDE
DIANA NAPIER · DERRICK de MARNEY
Directed by WALTER FORDE
"Jimmy Durante in the Best Musical in Town"
N. Y. World-Telegram
"Oscar Straus' most Lilting Score"
N. Y. Herald-Tribune
"Enjoyable Fare from First to Last"
N. Y. Times

SAMMY DAVIS, JR.

By the age of five, Sammy Davis, Jr. had learned the art of being an entertainer. He made the most of those years of experience and became one of the greats. In 1933 at the age of eight he appeared in two musical shorts, *Rufus Jones for President* and *Seasoned Greetings*. He found as he grew up (as all of us find) that film roles became harder to get when you are no longer an adorable kid. But his singing career took off with the Will Mastin Trio. Decca Records signed him to a contract in 1954.

In 1954 he lost his left eye in a severe car accident. After his unfortunate accident, nightclubs all over the country were clamoring for his services, so he returned to Ciros with his dad and uncle and they got one of the biggest ovations ever, 10 minutes, before the act even began! When he appeared on Broadway, critics raved about his "dynamism and unusual versatility." He became a huge hit on TV's *The Ed Sullivan Show*. As a recording artist he made dozens of top-selling albums and produced an all-time bestseller with "Candy Man," followed by "Hey There," "Birth of the Blues," "The Lady Is a Tramp," and "Who Can I Turn To."

Sammy truly advanced his fame when he joined the famous (or infamous) "Rat Pack," making several successful movies with its members including *Ocean's Eleven* (1960). His membership was a challenge because he had to compete with Frank Sinatra and Dean Martin to see who could get the biggest laughs.

HOLLYWOOD HOTWIRE

Hollywood Blvd. Gets a Facelift

SIDEWALK decorations on Hollywood bouevard are examined by (from left) Edwin L. Zabel, Actress Kip Hamilton, A. E. England, Councilman Earl D. Baker and E. M. Stuart, while Artist Jack Lane sketches a caricature of Cary Grant on the pavement. Seventy feet of sidewalk were painted and decorated for preview.
—Los Angeles Examiner photo.

Hollywood and Vine, 1959

A young hotwire who never quite made it to Secretary of State but who *was* a member of the Hollywood Chamber of Commerce, the next best bet, was someone I was exposed to in the '50s. He made the brilliant deduction that people who came all the way from Des Moines, Iowa, to see Hollywood were totally deflated. They would stand at the corner of Hollywood and Vine, look down the street, and they were looking at Des Moines, Iowa.

His plan was this: get the merchants to participate financially, to the tune of $7.5 million dollars, and then the Chamber of Commerce would move in, renovate all the storefronts, put the most modern city light fixtures up and have an island of tropical vegetation running down the middle of the entire boulevard. He would change the town completely. First of all, the sidewalks would be chocolate brown, with a yellow star every fourth square. In the star would be a caricature of some famous person from the movies, television and radio—2,000 faces in all. I would probably have had to return from Forrest Lawn to finish them up.

For three days and two nights, I was on my hands and knees painting the faces

Grauman's Chinese Theatre

in front of Grauman's Chinese Theatre so the Chamber members could see what it was going to look like. Their reaction? Great balls of fire—let's have at it. People were watching my every line, and one old guy hollered at me, "Is Francis X. Bushman going to be there?" I said, "Nope." He said, "Well then it won't be Hollywood." I didn't look up, but I'm sure it had been Francis X. doing the hollering. The project began to sink into quicksand because of the bickering over who was going to be on the key corner of Hollywood and Vine. At that point, the renovating of Hollywood fell on its keister when the merchants failed to come up with the pledged money and my Chamber of Commerce friend, who was railroading the whole magilla, bowed out fast. What they finally settled for years later were the embedded stars on Hollywood Boulevard that you see now, but you gotta admit that hardly measures up to miles and miles of brown and yellow sidewalks.

They finally settled on embedded stars.

MILTON BERLE

Any time he came into the Derby, Milton Berle *always* took a tour of the room and hobnobbed with everyone—whether he knew them or not. If they didn't make a good audience, he could always go home to his mother—she was the greatest one-woman audience ever. When Berle was playing vaudeville theaters he should have given his Mom top billing, because she was putting on a greater show out in the audience than he was onstage. To sit within three rows of her was a real experience in psychology. As soon as Miltie walked out on the stage, Mama came alive as though she had just awakened from a deep sleep. Whether it was four or five stage shows a day, she was out there for every one of them and she probably got the best rest she ever had sleeping through the movie between shows. When Berle told that first gag, she laughed hysterically and told everyone within hearing distance that was her son up there. If you were sitting next to her, you *had* to laugh at Milton to protect yourself, because if you didn't you got one of her flying elbows in the ribs. Berle never had to go home at night and say, "Ma, I did a lousy show today," because Mama was out there keeping a report card on him.

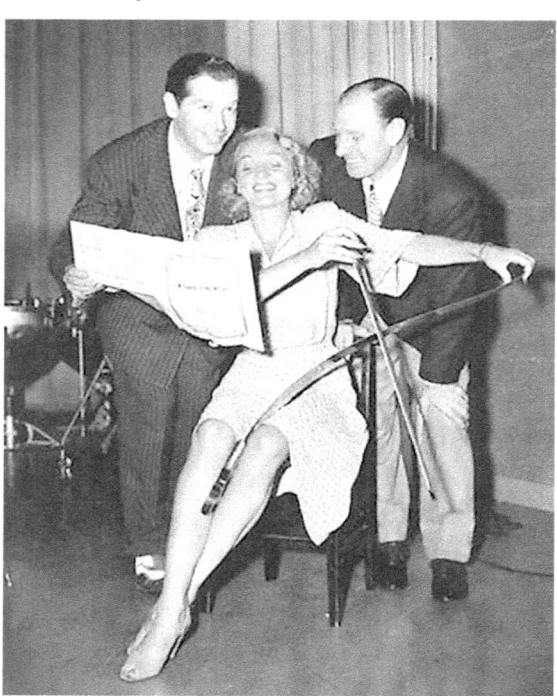

Marlene Dietrich, Milton Berle, Leo Durocher on Berle's radio show, June 1944

When television came into everyone's life, it turned out to be a mechanized version of vaudeville. Even the viewers were mechanized. They all piled into cars on a Tuesday night and drove over to the nearest poor sucker's house who owned a TV set, so they could watch Mr. Television on *The Milton Berle Show*. For more than six years, Berle kept people glued to their tube watching his antics and the tomfoolery of all the others with whom he was surrounded himself. He was probably responsible for more folks buying their own TV sets because they didn't like the brand of beer the guy whose house they invaded had served.

PETER LAWFORD

Hollywood has always had audiences all over the world. Its final epitaph will always be *Viva Le Audience!*

Le Audience was also a part of history of the Hollywood Brown Derby as well. The one night that the audience showed up automatically was Fight Night. Every Friday, the Hollywood American Legion Stadium, immediately behind the Derby, was the setting for fisticuffs demonstrated by such favorites as Maxie Rosenbloom and Art Aragon. Inside and outside the Derby it was standing room only. It was the one night that there were truly more movie stars in the Derby than there were in the heavens. The outside mobs were there to oooooh and aaaaah as each celebrity alighted from his car and entered the Derby. Permanent table reservations were in order—fervent fight fans like George Raft, Clark Gable, Carole Lombard, Lupe Velez and Mark Hellinger were there every Friday.

Fight Night was always the one evening Bob Cobb, the Derby owner, thoroughly enjoyed making his nightly round of the room, exchanging verbal tidbits with the famous and the frustrated. Bob was big on anything to do with athletics; he was a major stockholder in the Hollywood Stars baseball team, which played in the old Pacific Coast League. Consequently, he attracted many well-known pros to the Derby, who I had the honor of committing to paper for posterity: Bob Feller, Mickey Cochrane, Charlie Root (Cub pitcher famous for the Babe Ruth dirty finger pointing episode), Jimmy Demaret (golfdom's answer to Louis Roth), Bill Veeck, Fred Haney, Max Baer and Buddy Baer to name a few. Max, the heavyweight fighter who made like a playboy in the ring instead of out of it, had me do a copy of his caricature to send to his son, Max, Jr. Junior made a name for himself not throwing punches but throwing punch lines in *The Beverly Hillbillies* TV series.

Max Baer

On one of those Friday nights I was to go to a table where there were four gents sitting and I was to draw two of them. One was Peter Lawford and the other was someone I had never heard of before, Mack "Killer" Gray. It turns out he worked a lot with George Raft (rumor says as his bodyguard). He made over 41 films, usually in uncredited parts

or as thugs and bartenders. He played himself in George Raft's *Broadway* (1942). Carole Lombard supposedly gave him the nickname Killer. Of the other two guys sitting there, one had ordered oysters on the half shell and was taking them out of their shell and putting them in his hair, much to the amusement of the other guys. The other two were Jerry Lewis and Dean Martin. The Derby was bypassing them for the wall because they were only "nightclub comedians." It seemed like 20 minutes after that they became the two biggest names in show business. Even the Derby sometimes misjudged fame in the offing. Martin and Lewis kept cracking up my two subjects, making it tough to do the drawing.

But years later I got back at Dean Martin. He had me draw his caricature that was used as the sign for Dino's Restaurant on Sunset Blvd. He used the caricature on the menus, the napkins, and the advertising in the paper he did. I think he even had it tattooed on his chest.

That night when I drew Peter Lawford, film audiences everywhere knew who he was. Peter put on a lot of good mileage in Hollywood. He got off to a flying start in some pretty darned good company. Mickey Rooney and Freddie Bartholomew were doing a picture, *Lord Jeff* (1938) when Peter and his folks were visiting the set at MGM, which had been searching for an English boy. They offered the 15-year-old Peter the role, which he accepted. As a child he had had bit parts in two British films, *Poor Old Bill* (1930) and *A Gentleman of Paris* (1931).

However, his father, Sir Sidney, having retired as a Lieutenant General from the British army, and his mother, Lady Lawford, wanted to continue on their circling the globe endeavors and they needed Peter along to keep track of the Dramamine. They got hung up en route when WWII froze all their funds, so Peter had to give up his role of world traveler and settle down to parking cars. He saved enough money as a parking lot attendant to buy a one-way ticket to Hollywood. This may have been the wisest investment he ever made. To prove how you can turn popcorn into popularity, he worked as an usher at the Westwood Village Theatre, the same theater that screened many of his later hits. After an uncredited bit part as a pilot in the Academy Award-winning film, *Mrs. Miniver* (1942), all the studios put Lawford on the "wanted" list. After several successes he ended up back where he started, on the payroll at MGM. He went from *The White Cliffs of Dover* (1944) to *Mrs. Parkington* (1944) and *The Picture of Dorian Gray* (1945) to his first singing role with some guy by the name of Frank Sinatra and Jimmy Durante in *It Happened in Brooklyn* (1947). That probably earned him a membership in The Rat Pack…with such luminaries as Sinatra, Dean Martin, Sammy Davis, Jr. and Judy Garland. These were film stars having fun and games. Peter was always proud to list his occupation on a credit as "actor."

JOE E. BROWN

Joe E. Brown had the biggest mouth in Hollywood…and in the movie industry—and *that* really took some doing! It was said he couldn't cover his whole mouth when he yawned. But it sure paid to keep it open, because from the start of his career in 1928 until well into the '40s, he was among the 10 biggest box office attractions. He was always a big favorite with the kids when he opened that big yap and let loose that siren-like howl. It sounded just like the kids when they were letting loose in the schoolyard at recess. Joe always played the poor, hopeless, bungling soul who never does anything right but gets the big laugh. He was a firm believer in slapstick, which called for a lot of pratfalls. His early days spent as an acrobat in the circus had taught him that you either fall right or you are soon the proud owner of a slipped disc.

Joe loved baseball. Talk about putting clauses in a contract. He had one with Warner Bros. that put every free agent in baseball to shame. When it came time to sign the contract, Joe insisted that the studio have a complete ball team made up of company employees just for him. He wanted to be the Walter O'Malley of the movie world. Part of his fever was because he had been a part owner of the Kansas City Blues and for a short period, was the pre-game and post-game announcer for the New York Yankees.

One of the funniest bits he did in all the media (stage, movies, TV) was of a young rookie pitcher who was having a conniption fit on the mound while he tried to outguess the batters, sway the umpire and keep one eye on every base runner while the bases were loaded.

Although Joe put his money where his mouth was (and that took some doing because he was really making it by now), it was a trick that he did with his rubbery face that made his mouth look like a combination of the Grand Canyon and the Mammoth Cave. By throwing back his head so that his wide-open mouth would occupy the whole foreground of the audience's field of vision, he came

Jack Lemmon and Joe E. Brown on the set of *Some Like It Hot*

across looking like an oxygen tent with a split seam. Movie and TV cameramen always took full advantage of that shot.

His philosophy in life was love, learn and laugh. His last laugh in the movie *Some Like It Hot*, when after discovering his fiancée was really Jack Lemmon in drag he said, "Nobody's perfect!!" was one of the biggest he had ever received. Funny part is, that's what he said to me after I showed him the caricature I had done of him at the Derby!

HENRY KISSINGER

A gentleman who would more than likely prefer to forget the past was on the wrong side of one of my caricature karate kicks. Arlene Dahl gave a luncheon at the Derby for Henry Kissinger. He was then a member of Richard Nixon's staff and, of course, we had to mug Henry for the wall. I was really impressed when, immediately after being seated, Kissinger had a phone brought to the table and called San Clemente to "report in." It gave one a sense of security to know that, if we were invaded in the middle of my drawing, at least they knew where to get ahold of Henry to get him to the hiding place. Mr. Kissinger turned out to be a very charming and witty man and the last guy in the world you would think Mata Hari would want to be sleeping with. He kept

everyone at the table entertained with funnies that had happened at White House State dinners, such as the time he was seated next to Dean Rusk, then Secretary of State and at that time someone Kissinger didn't know all that well. The main course was served: lamb chops with panties. Then came the unexpected (something that could happen to the best of us). Henry was trying to cut one of his chops and the knife slipped and the chop flew off the plate and landed on Rusk's. Too embarrassed to mention to Dean he was being deprived of his main sustenance, Henry settled for the mashed potatoes and peas. Rusk, to this day, probably feels that because he was Secretary of State, the Good Lord recognized his rank and tossed him an extra bonus.

I hope Henry Kissinger realizes the important significance of having had his caricature on the wall of the Brown Derby, because it was shortly thereafter that he was appointed Secretary of State.

MICKEY ROONEY

Mickey Rooney (who was first Joe Yule, Jr.) was taking bows onstage from the time he was 18 months old. In his 80s now, he can still earn a standing ovation with some of his antics. In his heyday as a child star and then a young man, he reached his pinnacle by becoming moviedom's biggest attraction.

Rooney made the jump from appearing with his family in vaudeville to the big screen at six years of age. He immediately became a star in a comedy series billed Mickey McGuire beginning in 1927. He stole the name "Mickey" from that and came up with "Rooney" to make it his official name. In 1934 he began his career with MGM in *Manhattan Melodrama*, followed by the long-running and immensely popular Andy Hardy series. He moved on to *Boys Town* (1938) and then joined Judy Garland in several delightful musical motion pictures for which the duo earned fame. Their most popular entries were *Babes in Arms* (1939), *Strike Up the Band* (1940) and *Babes on Broadway* (1941).

He proved himself to be a polished character actor in such movies as *Baby Face Nelson* (1957) and in 1961 in *Breakfast at Tiffany's*. Sir Laurence Olivier, no piker as a legitimate actor himself, said, "Mickey Rooney was the best actor America had ever had." Mickey Rooney has appeared in over 233 films and is still working today.

Mickey Rooney and Judy Garland pose as they sign the cement at Grauman's in 1939.

NORMAN ROCKWELL

One of the most interesting sessions I had in drawing the celebrities' caricatures is when I became an artist drawing his version of another artist. The other artist was one of the most famous and popular artists of 20th-century American painters, and will be for generations to come—Norman Rockwell. He specialized in depicting idyllic scenes of small town and rural life. His illustrated covers for the *Saturday Evening Post* reached millions of people each week, and the public as well as media critics described every one of them as a classic. His 317 covers appeared from 1916 through 1963 and they included the "Four Freedoms" series that were reproduced as posters by the Office of War Information during WWII. Norman created drawings for the official Boy Scout calendars, the deluxe edition of *Tom Sawyer* as well as *Huckleberry Finn*, contributed to *Boys' Life, Judge, Literary Digest, Look* and other magazines. In 1977 he was awarded the Presidential Medal of Freedom.

I assured Norman I would put his caricature on the Wall of Fame at the Hollywood Brown Derby if he would draw me for the cover of the *Saturday Evening Post*, but he didn't buy that idea. I guess I was too good-looking for the characters he usually portrayed. (I lie a lot.)

One of the comments I often hear from people who are watching me draw someone is, "Whatta talent this guy has. I can't draw a straight line with a ruler." But at one time everyone could draw…and so could you, your spouse, your friends, your in-laws and your kids.

Everyone who arrives on this earth starts out as an artist. Give a kid a Crayola and he draws a house, a tree, stick figures of his parents…and then he really goes all out on coloring books. Go into any family restaurant and watch all of the little boys and girls sitting with their family while coloring

Norman Rockwell poses for me at the Derby.

away on placemats. The hamburger gets served and they are so wrapped up in their artistic efforts they ignore the food.

Then they get to be seven or eight years old and they throw the crayon away and that's it, brother. Thank goodness they didn't all follow through and become artists, or I would have so much competition I couldn't make a living at it.

DONALD O'CONNOR

When I drew Donald O'Connor I brought something to his attention that I'm sure he had never been aware of—that he had been a "mean widdle kid." Before I got my drawing talents into high gear, I had been a performer in vaudeville. As a matter of fact, I was one of its pallbearers. However, television resurrected vaudeville and gave it a new name...Ed Sullivan. Donald was also a member of the four-a-day, five-on-Saturday-and-Sunday profession as the youngest male of the O'Connor family. Those were the days of the funny-hat acts, and his brothers, both comedians, wore funny hats. When Donald would come onstage and proceed to steal the show with his "meanest kid in town" routine, his uncles would try to destroy this brat by hitting him over the head with their hats after every punch line. For spite, Donald would then practice his Dennis the Menace shtick by getting into the dressing rooms of the other acts on the bill and turning their $2.50 (big money then) boxes of powder makeup upside down. A funny kid onstage…a miserable one off.

When I reminded him of his dubious honor of being the first juvenile delinquent, he laughed and laughed. But then what could you expect from a guy who had never attended public school. The only education he was

getting was backstage but it was coming from the best teacher in the world, his mom Effie. She had put the O'Connor Family together and by gosh, the first thing she was going to teach them was how to earn their living in show business. The only thing Donald got cheated out of was a high school reunion, but those always turn out to be comparison parties where you find out who has gone through the most wives and who has lost the most hair.

Donald didn't confine his backstage education to just how to write his name on somebody else's blank check.

A pencil drawing I did of Donald O'Connor

Donald O'Connor in *Francis Goes to West Point*

He also picked up instructions in dancing: tap, buck and wing, the soft shoe and the double shuffle and there's not a vocational class in the school system that offers *that*! At the age of 13, O'Conner did a benefit performance at L.A.'s Biltmore Hotel and was signed up by a Paramount Pictures talent scout. The ink wasn't even dry on the contract when the studio dropped him because his voice changed. (He should have sued because *that* was an act of God!) You couldn't stop an O'Connor with a weak excuse like that—by 1950 Donald was voted the most versatile song and dance man in movies. The only competition he ran into who could almost steal a picture from him was a trained mule, Francis, but between the two of them, their pictures grossed millions at the box office.

One of Donald's most memorable dance routines was the one he did in the MGM film, *Singin' in the Rain* (1952), starring another fast on his feet man, Gene Kelly. The sequence showed up again in the more modern movie, *That's Entertainment!* and was classified by all as "wild, man, wild." When I drew Donald O'Connor I was in the habit of wearing a smock in the Derby to protect my Jim Clinton suit from flying soup stains and, from then on, every time Donald came into the Derby and saw me walking the aisles, he would holler, "Here comes the schmuck in the schmock!"

OMAR SHARIF

In today's world, nobody seems to be all that happy with what they're doing, so sometimes it pays to just assume a whole new role in life. At the Derby I drew just such a person—the last one you would ever suspect of having such a desire. It was Omar Sharif, who longed to be "just another guy like your friendly credit dentist." And isn't that life for you? The friendly credit dentist would give his favorite set of molars to be Omar Sharif. Omar said he had had it with being put on a pedestal as "the great lover," a reputation he has been asked many times to live up to—and one time at the point of a gun. As he tells it, he was staying in a hotel in Dallas and the word had gotten out that "Wow! Omar Sharif was on the premises." This particular night, he retired to his room, "pajamaed-up" and went "beddy-bye." At 2 a.m., he was startled by a raucous knocking at his door and, when he opened it, thinking the hotel was being evacuated because of a fire or something, he was confronted by a very drunken woman in a dead mink stole with a very live .45 in her hand. She entered the room and demanded that Omar strip to the gills and make love to her. The more he tried to reason with her, the more insistent became her demands. He finally convinced her that staring down the barrel of a mean-looking revolver does absolutely nothing to stimulate the sex hormones, so she turned on her heels, bellowed out in her best alcoholic *basso profundo*, "You Hollywood faggots are all alike," and slammed the door.

She was slamming the door on a man who has the distinction of being the only Egyptian to become a top-flight, world-renowned movie star. Born in Alexandria of wealthy Lebanese and Syrian parents, he was raised and educated speaking only the French language. He studied acting at Victoria

Peter O'Toole, Gamil Ratib and Omar Sharif in *Lawrence of Arabia*

College in Cairo, but condescended to join his father's timber business after graduating. That was good for about 20 minutes because at the first chance to act, he flew the coop from Daddy's biz.

Under the name "Omar el Cherif" he appeared in many Egyptian films, none of which were seen outside of Arab countries. In the early 1960s, someone touted him to David Lean as the ideal actor to play Sherif Ali Ibn Kharish in *Lawrence of Arabia* (1962). The "tout" turned out to be a wise one, because Omar won a Best Supporting Actor nomination for an Oscar and a contract with Columbia Pictures. Omar is actually a walking International House of Pancakes because he has played any kind of nationality you can mention. He's been an American, a Spanish priest, Yugoslav, and even a Russian in *Doctor Zhivago* (1965), a movie that critics disliked and the public loved. It was an immense financial success and still draws a crowd in TV reruns. From 1966 through 1968, Omar was one of the busiest actors on the premises. He has a very simple way of going about it. He says, "No matter who I play…it's me. If a director or producer wants Omar Sharif to play a part, that's what he gets, Omar Sharif. All I care about is getting to the studio on time and remembering my lines."

Geraldine Chaplin and Omar Sharif in *Doctor Zhivago*

Omar loves to tell of how he represented Egypt, as their champion bridge player, in the 1964 Olympic Bridge Tournament. At this point, he's content to play a little bridge, ride a few horses, handpick the roles that appeal to him, and his big kick in life is to double-date with his son—who incidentally, was the little "winner" in *Dr. Zhivago*, who in the film played his father at age 8.

DANNY THOMAS

When it comes to dropping your original name, Danny Thomas must have been first in line. He was probably 21 before he learned how to spell his given name, sometimes listed as Amos Muzyad Jahoob and other times as Muzyad Yahkoob and even Amos Jacobs. No wonder he was confused. When you're born you take whatever name they gave you, but when they hang one like that on you, even though it's Lebanese, I'm sure he spent his childhood looking through the book of names. Even at that, when he started his career as a stand-up comedian, the best he could come up with was Amos Jacobs. After several nightclub bookings, he switched his name to the one we all know best, Danny Thomas. While appearing at one of the better clubs in Chicago, he was discovered by Abe Lastfogel, who was the head of the William Morris Agency. Abe was so impressed by Thomas' comedic talent that he booked him on a USO tour that included Marlene Dietrich, and then got him a shot on Fanny Brice's radio show. This resulted in him being named the "Best Newcomer in Radio." The movie bigwigs wanted Danny to get a $50 nose job but he refused and still made a big hit in *The Jazz Singer* (1953) and with Doris Day in *I'll See You In My Dreams* (1951).

When television became a part of everyone's life. Danny jumped on the bandwagon. He staggered through several shows that just weren't Danny Thomas at his best, when he dreamed up a concept that had become the story of his own life. He had been on tour so much that he almost had to reintroduce himself to his kids when he got home. To keep their mommy, Rose Marie, from being lonesome they piled into bed with her every night but when Daddy was due home they had to clear out and "make room for Daddy." He sold ABC on the idea and it became one of the most successful shows on television running from 1953 though 1964.

Just to prove to the world that he had the know-how when it came to producing, Danny joined with director Sheldon Leonard in creating such great shows as *The Real McCoys, The Andy Griffith Show, The Joey Bishop Show*, and *The Dick Van Dyke Show*. Danny set an example for Hollywood and all of us to follow; that is, there are more important things in life than just being an overwhelming success. In 1962 he founded the St. Jude's Research Hospital, which has cured many catastrophic children's diseases. For that we will always remember Danny Thomas.

JACK LANE: THE BEGINNING

I started out my career as a portrait artist and these samples are from my high school days. As you can see, I was unknowingly drawing celebrities even in those days. Because I loved this caricaturist's work so much, I adopted a hero, Roy Nelson, who was with the *Chicago Daily News*. Roy could distort a face to the hilt, but you knew exactly who it was supposed to be. I will always contend he was the best in the business. When I graduated from school, thinking I would like to get a job with a newspaper, I made an appointment to show Roy my efforts. He looked at a few of my caricatures and said, "Hey! Those are my ears!" He always drew an ear as a half moon circle and then put a small curved line in the middle. I had admired his stuff so much I shoplifted his ear action. His editor and Roy both told me there were no real opportunities for an artist in the newspaper field.

So with that hard fact to face up to, I got myself into playing vaudeville theaters and drawing other performers who were on the bill. My greatest training came from drawing my fellow G.I.s in the army. I loved those odd faces. For a caricature, they were my kind of folks.

Here I am in the Army now, clowning around in a camp variety show.

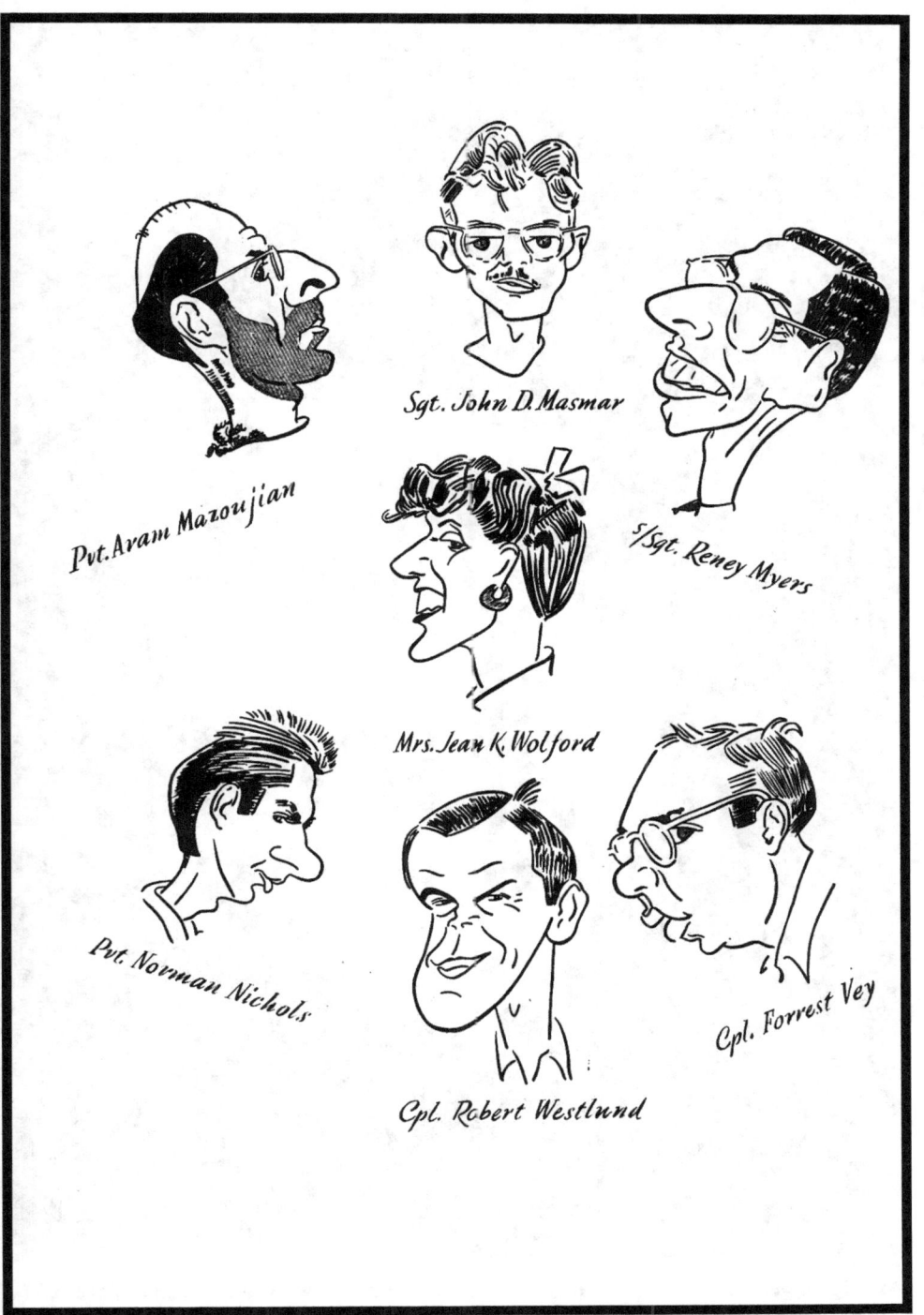

Some of my fellow G.I.s gave me my greatest training!

As a teenaged horror movie fan I tried my hand at drawing Boris Karloff from *The Black Cat*.

This is the original photograph from *The Black Cat* that I used for my drawing.

Lon Chaney, Sr.

Lon Chaney, Sr. with his famous makeup case

F.D.R.

Another F.D.R. portrait

Adolphe Menjou

Adolphe Menjou always played the suave sophisticate in films such as *Stage Door*. He once remarked, "It was my mustache that landed jobs for me. In those silent-film days it was the mark of a villain. When I realized they had me pegged as a foreign nobleman type I began to live the part too. I bought a pair of white spats, an ascot tie and a walking stick."

Lewis Stone's hair turned gray when he was in his 20s, thus he was usually cast as characters much older then himself. Stone fought in the Spanish-American War and was in the cavalry in WWI (which probably helped him out in all those Westerns he appeared in such as *Three Godfathers*). He is most remembered as kindly Judge Hardy in the successful Mickey Rooney-MGM series.

DR. CHARLES LOWMAN

The oldest gentleman I ever drew in my born days was as keen and alert as an old-time fire station dog when the bell started clanging and was a true gentleman in every sense of the word. It was 97-year-old Doctor Charles Lowman: founder of the Los Angeles Orthopedic Hospital, "Doctor of the Century" in 1971, and recipient of the nation's highest citizen's award, the Medal of Freedom, in 1974. He was distinguished for his work among the survivors of the San Francisco earthquake in 1906. He also served in WWI as a Medical Corps captain. Written up in the *Los Angeles Times* for his humanitarian efforts, Dr. Lowman told me he had treated over 46,000 patients in his time.

I asked him if he still made house calls, for which he gave me his best professional fish eye. I felt I was going to have to have a bottle of plasma handy while I drew him, but the good doctor turned out to be a very alert, sharp-minded individual who carried his 97 years like a man of 65.

As I sketched away, a friend at his table said to him, "Doctor…to what do you attribute your successfully reaching this age?" The good doctor picked up a knife on the table, held it up for all to see, and said, "You have to keep your mind as sharp as this knife"…which should be a lesson for all of us to keep our blades whet!

A large factor in Dr. Lowman's longevity was his great sense of humor. A friend tells of how, when Charles was about to re-marry at the age of 90, he asked this friend if he would help him out on his wedding night. Kiddingly, the friend said "Of course." As the time drew near, Dr. Lowman asked him again if he would help him out on his wedding night. (You remember that he was 90 at the time.) Again, his friend reassured him, but then, when he asked the day prior to the wedding, his friend, getting a little leery, said, "What do you want me to do?" Dr. Lowman replied, "Will you carry my bride over the threshold, my back is killing me."

Charles really enjoyed my caricature of him, so I knew at this stage of his life his ego had slipped off into oblivion.

JOHNNY GRANT

To walk into the Brown Derby for the very first time in your life with Bob Hope's shirt, Dorothy Lamour's sarong and Jack Benny's shorts under your arm, is really making some kind of an entrance. Such was the case of Johnny Grant, Hollywood's Honorary Mayor. Johnny arrived here in 1944 wearing Uncle Sam's khaki clothes on what was billed as the World's Longest Treasure Hunt. The Lost Battalion had come home to the States and Wichita Falls, Texas, was planning a slam-bang old-fashioned Texas celebration. Part of the program was to auction off stars' items to raise money for war bonds, so John and his Army buddy flew out in a B-25 to get their hands on whatever they could. Bob Burns got a little too enthused with the project and gave the boys a Berkshire pig. It wouldn't have been so bad, but going back, the pig refused to wear a parachute and kept honking for a hostess. But talk about being piggish. Some guy wouldn't stop bidding at the auction until he had pledged $300,000 for it...and it didn't even look like Miss Piggy. The sarong brought $300,000 and Benny's shorts fell short because they didn't even have a fly in them, so they only went for $40,000. Altogether, Grant's excursion to the West Coast netted over $1,300,000.

Johnny Grant was master of ceremonies at the debut of the Cary Grant postage stamp.

It was while Johnny was in Hollywood fulfilling this assignment that he had the opportunity to mingle with the stars at luncheon in the Derby. He had heard so much about the place and it had lived up to his every expectation. His later visits to the Derby were when he was doing what everyone else was doing after the war...looking for a job. He knew Eddie Bracken from New York and at the time Eddie was quite successful in films and dined at the Derby regularly. Grant used to time it so he would arrive just as dessert was being served, and he would thrive on the only thing he could afford, a 25-cent piece of strawberry cream pie. Johnny claims he always left a small tip, but this is hard to believe because he had to snatch a little old lady's purse to get the quarter for the pie.

He finally got into some disc jockey jobs of the "midnight to four a.m." variety. He

Johnny Grant on tours for the USO.

Postcard from the American Forces Vietnam Network. Soldiers could send a request to Johnny Grant's Small World post office and they would receive postcards with photos of popular stars.

didn't have too many sober listeners, but the lushes loved him. Johnny had gotten to meet Bob Hope along the way, and he was in Hope's office one day when a call came in from March Field asking Hope if he could come down and entertain the "inmates." Bob had played there before and had a booking that would interfere, so he said to Johnny "You know the gags as well as I do…why don't you get a group and go out there?" It was the beginning of a long USO jaunt for Johnny Grant that took him on 43 overseas tours and to half of the camps in the United States. You had to be on the alert doing stand-up comedy for the Viet Nam and Korean G.I.s because they had seen and heard Hope, Berle and Don Rickles on TV. If you weren't funny, you were liable to get turned over to the enemy.

The beauty of the USO shows was the time that the individual G.I. unknowingly invested in them. First he would hear about the camp show coming, he would discuss it in anticipation with his buddies, write home about it and then knock his brains out trying to get his hands on some Kodak film. The day would finally come, he would spend hours in line, or wait for hours because he wanted a good seat and got there early. The show would come on, the pictures of the dancing girls were shot, and then he would become the entertainment critic for the *Army Times* by telling his buddies what was good and what was bad about the show. This was always followed by the beef with the G.I. who claimed he was a close friend or an in-law of the star of the show. All in all, it gave them something to hope for and made for great relief from all the drastic and tragic things that were happening around them.

Johnny now, in addition to being Honorary Mayor, is involved with community projects such as the Police and Fire Commission, heading up the yearly Santa Claus Parade along with Chamber of Commerce leaders and appearing nightly interviewing stars on his KTLA *Johnny Grant in Hollywood* show. As the "Honorary Mayor," he emcees all of the star ceremonies including the placing of a new name on Hollywood's sidewalks.

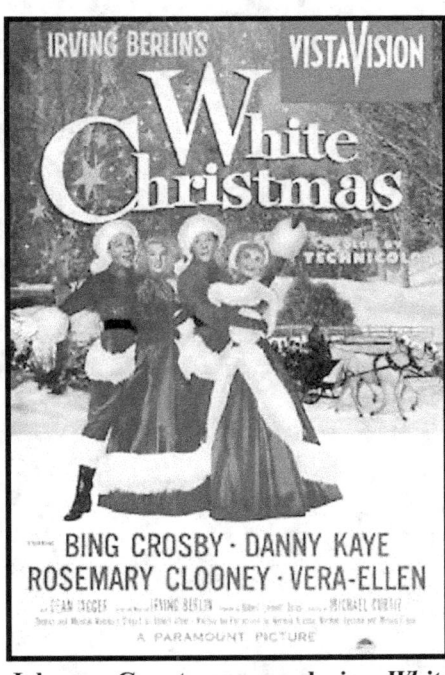

Johnny Grant appeared in *White Christmas* as TV host Ed Harrison.

145

BOB FELLER

Throwing a baseball by him at 100 miles per hour is the quickest way there is to get a batter's attention (and to turn a rough, tough umpire into a chicken). That was Bob Feller's hobby, his business and his ticket to fame. Anyone who strikes out over a thousand guys standing up there with that club on their shoulder has either got to have one great arm or he's using an electronic slingshot. Bob was only 16 when the Indians got word by smoke signal of the fabulous arm on this kid—"He struck out 18 batsmen in a seven-inning game." Even before Cleveland had his name on a contract (at his age they didn't even check his credit application), Feller had struck out eight of nine St. Louis Cardinals in an exhibition game.

In 1937 and 1938 he spent more time on the mound than any pitcher in the game and broke many records. He was either strikin' 'em out or walkin' 'em. He was so wild fans wouldn't purchase a box seat unless a mask and a chest protector went with the ticket. The challenge to the batter wasn't to hit the ball—but to keep from getting killed by it. As Bob said, "I just reared back and let them go." In 1940 Feller pitched 31 complete games and led the American League in strikeouts (263). In the winter of 1940 the *Sporting News* named Bob Feller the Number One Major League Baseball Player.

Bill Dickey, the Yankee catcher, once said, "His fastball looks like an aspirin tablet coming up to the plate only not quite as large." After I drew this caricature of Bob, I left the table fast before he picked up a cube of sugar and imbedded it in my skull at 110 miles per hour. I wonder what kind of gas mileage he got with that speed?

RESIDENT CARICATURIST

In my business of drawing caricatures, I'm strictly a face man. The thing that keeps my job so interesting is the fact that every face is different—there are no two the same! There are look-alikes, but no exact duplicates—and ain't we lucky—you could look like that guy next door! I have drawn what were supposed to be exact twins but, when they sit for me, one always has a feature that's a little bit different than the other: a bigger chin, a straighter nose, whatever, but it always shows up when you really study them. Speaking of look-alikes, I don't know how many guys I've drawn who think they look like Robert Redford or gals who swear they're an exact double for a young Liz Taylor, and then they see their drawing and their pipedream goes down the drain. I don't call my sketches "ego busters" for nothing!

Marjorie Rambeau and Ann Blyth in *Slander* (1956)

One person I drew at the Derby who didn't hold back any punches was the old English actress, Marjorie Rambeau. She taught me that "what a woman says is not what she means." I also learned that when you draw women in that age bracket you are playing Russian roulette with a loaded pencil. As I was dropping her lines on the paper, I could see this was all a mistake, so I said to her, "Now you realize this is a caricature." In her best British accent she replied, "Don't worry about it. I understand perfectly well what you are doing." A few more lines in critical places and I cowered at what I saw shaping up, so I said, "Is there a place you can go lie down after you see this?" She said, "Don't be of concern. I have a grand sense of humor! Just finish it and we'll both have a good laugh." That got my courage up, so I held it up for her to see—and she put a new hole in the ceiling of the Derby! She zoomed straight up á la Clark Kent in one of his most stirring rescues. Talk about blowing your wig! That was the closest I ever came to getting my eyes scratched out and having my shingle "Resident Caricaturist" stuffed in my left ear.

My victims were always riding me for something of which I am proud. I am the only left-to-right artist in the history of art. Can I help it if, when I picked up that matchbox cover that said "Draw Me" and I sent it in, the guy on the box was facing left to right? Whenever they sit for me and want

MARJORIE RAMBEAU

to be drawn the other way, I tell them to get a left-handed artist. Even with my drawings on the walls of the Derby, I got trapped to the point where Groucho Marx used to say, "It looks like everybody's lookin' out the door to see who's comin' in." I always do about a three-quarter profile, because it would surprise you, especially for a caricature, to see how many bumps in the nose and recesses of the chin (or chins, as in plural) show up. Unless a person has a very unusual construction to their face, like their nose is on sideways or their eyes look like they're buried in bags, they just don't lend themselves to a good caricature head-on.

Years ago when I was in show business, I drew Jack Teagarden, the famous trombonist, and I felt he came up with a classic when he voiced his disillusionment with my sketch. He said, "You made my nose look like an old bicycle seat!" And it was true, because that's what his nose really looked like—an old bicycle seat.

Louis Prima also proved that ego isn't confined to just your everyday egomaniac. His drummer wanted to put the caricature I drew of Louie on the face of his big drum, but Prima put the kibosh on that. His face already looked like it had been beat on without the drummer stompin' on it with his foot pedal.

Woody Herman, Spike Jones and Frankie Carle accepted their pencil punishment gracefully, as did Glenn Miller, whom I drew while I was in New York. He had newspaper mats made of his and sent them out as publicity releases, which fed my ego to no end.

You would be amazed at how many people who sit for me say, "Oh, that's the worst side of my face." I tell them the only good side to their head is the back of it, and I'm not going to draw that. This is a carryover from when everyone was brainwashed by the screen mags about how the stars would only allow themselves to be filmed or photographed from one side and how the lighting was such as to hide all the defects the vicious camera could spot. Now everybody is convinced they've got one good side to their face, in spite of what I keep trying to tell them with my best Don Rickles delivery.

In the world of caricature, I'm not what you would refer to as a "photo fan." My mode of drawing is to have the person sit for me for as long as it takes to capture their features. In most cases, it means about a 10- to 15-minute sitting, unless they have an exceptionally bad head, and then it takes until Friday (of next week—and I have had some of those). The beauty of having them sitting in front of me is that everything is laid out in the raw!

But there have been times when I have had no choice. I had to work from photos—and these were cases where the ol' debbil EGO was raising its ugly

Louis Prima

Woody Herman

Spike Jones

Hedda Hopper

head—again! Gals like Louella Parsons, Sheilah Graham and Hedda Hopper had been using their high school graduation pictures at the top of their column for years. There was no way they were going to concede to the public that they too, like us, were falling victim to the aging process. As far as they were concerned, aging was strictly for cheese and George Burns. So when it

I did this portrait for Rosalind Russell.

came time for them to join our hanging family, they wanted no part of Jack Lane and his poison pencils. They handed me the same photograph they had used for identification purposes— when they were volunteer nurses in WWI. To say that I was frustrated is hardly a play on words. I drew Hedda as she looked in her 30s, put a beautiful hat on her and, when she autographed it (which was part of our ritual), she said it was the best likeness she had ever seen of herself. This was like putting Unguentine ointment on my hurting guilt complex.

I think the most redeeming feature of anyone's face is the smile. You wouldn't believe the number of faces I've drawn where a good smile would kill 'em. You know what the man upstairs said, "No matter how hard you try, you can't use up all your smiles in a lifetime." A lot of people give up smiling because, when they do, all they have to offer is a beautiful set of "tooth." I have thrown in as much as $400 worth of dental work on a sketch, and never charged them a cent.

One thing we seem to lose sight of is that God wasn't running a beauty contest when He put us on this earth. Most of us got the usual number of eyes, ears and noses, and so it wouldn't be monotonous that we look at somebody else and see ourselves, the good Lord mixed up the patterns a little. Some of us came out looking like a crazy quilt, but what the Hell—as long as you're healthy. When it comes to beauty, most people have 20-20 vision anyway—20 inches out of each eye.

In the look-alike department, there was a funny but typical incident that happened to Derby wall newcomer, Richard Sherman of the Sherman Brothers, who wrote "Super-cali-fragi-listic-expi-ali-docious" for the Disney film *Mary Poppins*. They won an Academy Award for "Chim Chim Cher-ee" from the same film that year and, of course, appeared on television accepting their Oscars.

Now Richard is a carbon copy in the "looks" department to Walter Matthau, and a short time after doing his winning walk-on for the Oscar show, he was standing in a hotel lobby in Vegas when a woman ran up and

Academy Award-winning composers Robert and Richard Sherman

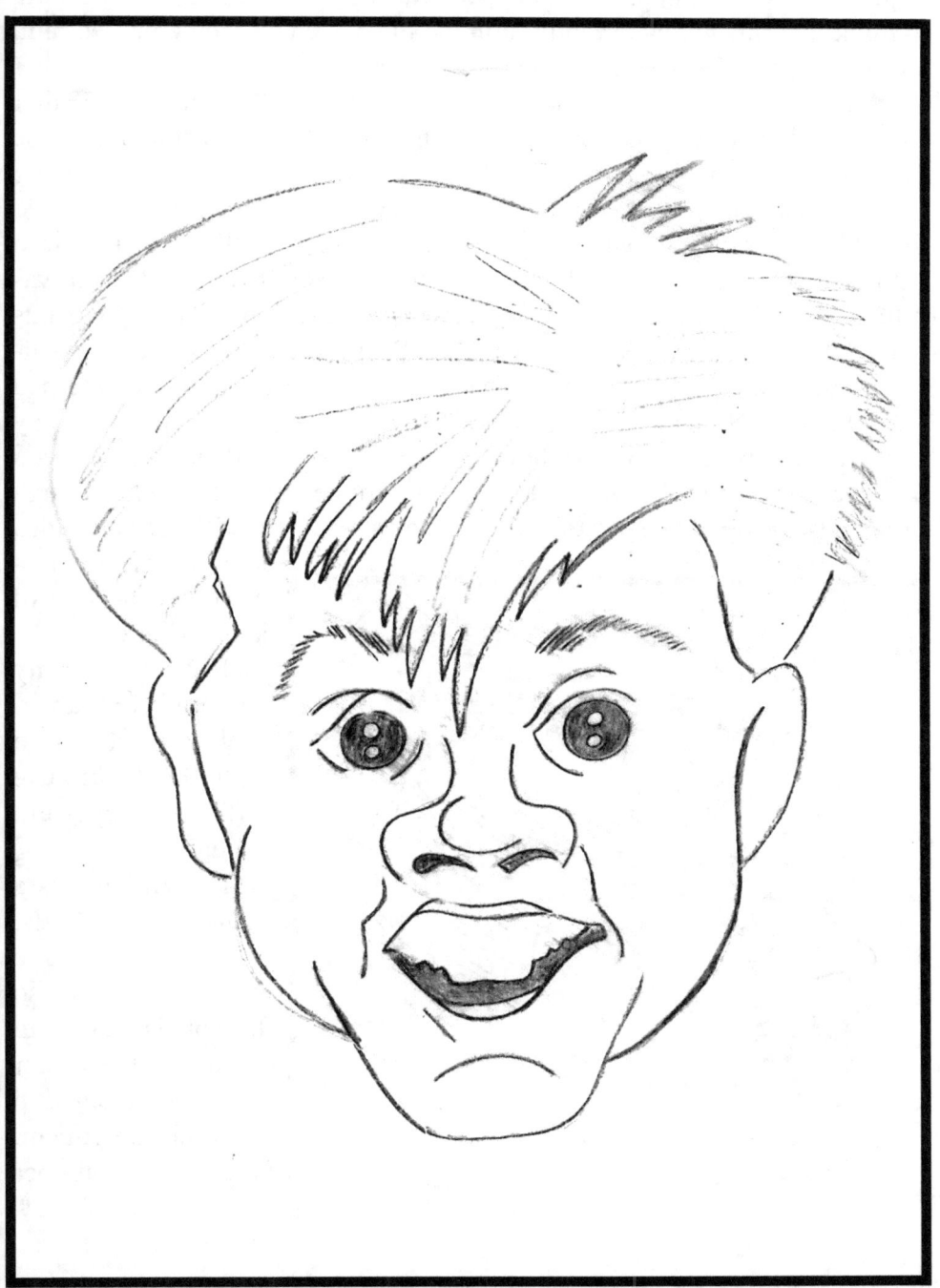

This pencil drawing of Mickey Rooney features what I consider the most redeeming feature of anyone's face—the smile.

requested his autograph. This pumped Richard's ego into the *tilt* position, to think that this gal had seen him on the big screen and remembered him, so he whipped off his John Hancock in his best penmanship and handed her the slip of paper. She took one look at it and said, "Oh, you're not Walter Matthau," threw the paper on the floor and stalked away, just another case of the frustrated public duping itself.

People are anxious to see, talk to or touch a celebrity, again just to feed that old insatiable ego, so they can tell their friends, "You'll never guess who I stood next to—and he called me Cupid!" What he probably called her was "stupid," but the ego has a great capacity for hearing things the way it wants to hear them. In my stint at the Hollywood Brown Derby, I saw the stars suffer through a meal trying to get two mouthfuls of hot soup in before it turned ice cold while they had to carry on an inane conversation with somebody from Ames, Iowa, "whose nephew has a daughter and looks just like you did when you were a baby." After being interrupted for autographs through the appetizer, the entrée and the dessert, they stagger out of the Derby with a case of heartburn that even Pepto Bismol couldn't cure.

Believe me, my caricature had absolutely nothing to do with the traumatic suffering they went through.

Eve Arden was a frequent diner at the Brown Derby. She was usually alone, so she would invite me to sit and chat with her while she indulged in the food department. She was my number one gal in the friendship department.

Eve Arden

Dorothy Lamour indulges in a sweet treat at the Brown Derby (Photofest)

FRANCIS X. BUSHMAN

But the topper was Francis X. Bushman. By the time the Derby decided to do him, he was pressing 75—to the wall! In his mind, there was only one lifelong image of Francis X.—and that was as the star of *Ben-Hur* (1925). Charlton's might as well have been called "The Son of Ben-Hur." The photo of Francis was so old it was turning gray. Therefore, once again I took 50 years off his current driver's license and did a Houdini on paper. I felt like God, knocking off all those years on these people. Without realizing it, I probably invented the first facelift! Later when Francis was in his 80s, I had him as my guest on a TV show I was doing. I told him I would introduce him as "one of the first great Movie Idols." In no uncertain terms, he informed me: "I was not *one* of the first—I was *the* first," thereby proving that the "ham bone is connecta to da ego bone!"

He got reflecting back to the days when he was making money as fast as they were printing it—and with no taxes yet. At that time, all of the major motion picture studios were located in the heart of Hollywood, or at least near Hollywood and Vine, which has always been its hub. A Realtor approached Francis in the Brown Derby and offered him a piece of property (where Mann's Chinese Theatre now sits) for $20,000. At this point in his career, that wouldn't have even nudged his income, but Francis turned down the deal because the location was "too far away." This was maybe two miles from Hollywood and Vine. Years later, he asked Sid Grauman the value of the property (after the theater was already built and the stars' feet and handprints were a tourist's challenge to try on for size), and Sid told him it was valued at two and a half million. It was the first time in Sid's life that he had to stand there and watch a grown man cry.

Francis X. Bushman in *Ben-Hur*

Actually, tears were coming easy for Francis X. about this time. For 15 years in silent films he had received worldwide adulation, but when he played the mighty Messala in *Ben-Hur*, the greatest picture of his career, his appeal diminished perceptibly. From that moment on, he was relegated to playing in serials like *Dick Tracy* and being featured in B films. His last picture,

FRANCIS X. BUSHMAN

THE FIRST BEN HUR

The Ghost in the Invisible Bikini (1966), didn't even rate a B. It was a C movie…and this is like the kiss of death in the business. But you can't keep a good ego down, so Bushman just tilted his nose a little higher and went on living in the past.

LOUIS JOURDAN

If you were ever dining in the Hollywood Brown Derby trying to spot a celebrity and you noticed a good-looking guy staring intently at you, you didn't have to worry that he was sizing you up for a mugging. He was just indulging in his favorite pastime of "people watching," looking to see if you had any characteristics he could add to one of his portrayals. The handsome harvester of traits would be Louis Jourdan. Louis has always worked to establish himself as an actor rather than be looked upon as just a type—accented, dark, manly, Continental, who kisses women's hands just to prove that he is a Frenchman.

Jourdan was destined to have some sort of career in films because his father was one of the promoters of the Cannes Film Festival. Louis evidently didn't spend much time looking in the mirror because his first efforts in the industry were as an assistant director.

It took his close friends to convince him that he was probably the best-looking guy in Paris and that he should become an actor. Not only did he change the direction of his career, but he changed his name from Pierre to Louis to play opposite Charles Boyer in his first movie *Le Corsaire* (1939).

Louis Jourdan in *The Paradine Case* (1947)

He was beginning to come on strong and had an assignment to make a film in Rome when war between Italy and France broke out. When his country fell to the Nazis, Louis was forced to join a work gang to cut wood, dig ditches and to help build roads. After a year of this, Jourdan was permitted to report back to the studios in occupied France. They were being allowed to make films but Louis was warned he would only be sanctioned to appear in non-political cinemas.

Louis Jourdan

However, what was being shot just turned out to be propaganda, so he managed an escape and rejoined his family. The Gestapo immediately arrested his father and Jourdan turned to the French underground to help his people. He was assigned to carry messages for the resistance and to help print anti-

German leaflets, both jobs considered crimes punishable by death. Louis did his job and was alert enough to avoid the German patrols but after the Liberation, he ran into a crowd of enemy soldiers who proceeded to beat him.

After France once again became a free country, Louis went back to the film industry in Paris. A talent scout, sensing that he had a new discovery for U.S. motion picture fans, sent some clips to David O. Selznick. David sent for Jourdan and gave him the big Hollywood royal treatment, signing him for his first picture *The Paradine Case* (1947). Selznick and Louis fought constantly over the insipid lover roles that Jourdan was being assigned, so between suspensions from the studio, Jourdan did a Broadway show, several films in France, and a successful French TV series.

He almost turned down the role that earned him the most attention. When they were casting for *Gigi*, Lerner and Lowe wanted Louis as the Parisian *bon vivant* Gaston, but the part called for some singing and he felt his singing in the bathroom baritone would never do. It was only after he cut a test record that even he was convinced he could get away with it.

People often ask me who was the handsomest man I have ever drawn and I always come up with "Louis Jourdan"—and he's still a people-watcher. Now he watches people from the wall of the Disney version of the Hollywood Brown Derby in Florida.

VICTOR BORGE

If you happen to be attending your own funeral and the organist turns out to be one of the funniest guys around, you're going to have to mind your manners and not start giggling or you'll spoil the whole affair for your friends. I'm sure he only indulged in that hobby once in awhile, but Victor Borge did play the organ at a few select funerals. This was only one of the many facets of his tremendous talents, which included actor, composer, pianist, writer, director of stage, screen, radio shows and he was even a flyer. Victor was a fun guy to draw because he was a walking one-liner. He loved to put a "topper" on everything else anyone said. There is one word that described his humor to a T—spontaneous! He may have started out on stage with a smattering of a routine but the longer he was on, the more adlibbed his act became.

Borge got a running start as a concert pianist but he couldn't restrain his wit and in no time the playing of the piano became secondary to his comedy routines. When Germany invaded Denmark, Victor and his wife were fortunate enough to get out, arriving in the United States in 1940. He was still a funny man but only in Swedish, French and German. His English was still incognito. Victor spent months sitting in movie theaters repeating the actor's dialogue coming off the screen. I'm sure he was told many times by ushers he was interrupting the enjoyment of the other patrons by talking aloud to himself, but it did work. He had a chance to audition for Rudy Vallee but Rudy only wanted to use him to warm up his studio audience before the Vallee radio show went on the air. Hearing about him, Bing Crosby signed Borge up for a guest appearance on his radio show and Victor killed the audience. The switchboard was lit up for a week with people calling to find out who the kook was who broke them up the other night. With that kind of response, Borge was made a regular on Crosby's *Kraft Music Hall* and remained for 56 weeks. His most talked about routine with the listening public was his "phonetic punctuation," a piece of material that no comedian has ever been able to successfully steal.

Victor moved with ease into the posh nightclub circuit and in no time, was one of its highest paid entertainers. After a couple of movies, Borge got back on more familiar ground and began broadcasting *The Victor Borge Show* on NBC, but his appeal on radio was nothing compared to the success he enjoyed on television and in concert. To thoroughly appreciate Victor you had to see him in action.

After our drawing session, he autographed a book he had written called *My Favorite Intermissions*, and gave it to me to show he wasn't really going to kill me for my caricature of him. Maybe mutilate—but not kill.

ESTHER WILLIAMS

"Wet she is a star…dry she ain't." Of course that was only Fanny Brice's opinion of Esther Williams, who during 1949 and 1950, was the biggest moneymaking female star second only to Betty Grable. And the funny part is, she really didn't want to be a star. She never thought of herself as an actress and most of the critics agreed with her. Esther just wanted to be what she appeared to be to everyone who saw her—an All American girl with natural beauty, vitality and vivaciousness, who when she dove into a swimming pool, made Johnny Weissmuller look like the Incredible Hulk.

Esther loved that water so much that even as a kid, she worked to get into it. When she was eight years old, a public playground pool was built near her home, largely through the efforts of her mom's P.T.A. activities. Mother had worked hard to get it there, but she just wasn't going to turn Esther loose to spend her life underwater. You want to practice belly flops—you earn it. So Esther took on the dull task of counting towels—one hour of swim time for every 100 towels. That job would be nonexistent today, because you couldn't get a towel at a public pool if your life depended on it. Just remember, every time you saw Esther Williams in the water, a counted towel got her there. She showed her determination to be a great swimmer when the coaches at the Los Angeles Athletic Club told her that if she doubled up on her efforts, she could become a champion within four years. Esther was 15 at the time and four years sounded like forever. She told them, "I can't wait that long. I'll do it in two or not at all." That she did! In 1938 she broke the world record in her lap of the 880-yard relay at the Senior National Championships in Santa Barbara.

Esther poses for a studio portrait in 1947

Handsome Ricardo Montalban shows romantically what he feels about curvaceous Esther Williams. Esther seems willing.

Later, in Des Moines, she shattered the record for the 100-meter freestyle and was the outstanding member of the champion 200- and 400-meter relay teams. That same year she also set a record for the 100-meter breaststroke. The Des Moines Nationals were actually the tryouts for the Olympics that were to be held in Helsinki, Finland, and with her record setting, Esther was on her way to swimming for the American flag in the victory lap at the world's greatest sports event. A thing called war canceled the 1940 Olympics. Medals didn't put food on the table and by themselves didn't taste all that good, even with salt and pepper, so Esther had to face getting out of the water, drying herself off, and going out and getting a job. She was pretty enough to get immediately hired at Magnin's as a model.

Opportunity knocked and Esther had her eye at the keyhole, so she let him in. "Him" turned out to be Billy Rose, who was planning the Aquacade at the San Francisco World's Fair, and he had heard all about this lovely champion swimmer from California. He made her an offer she couldn't refuse, so she tossed her amateur standing into the deep end of the pool, turned pro, and became the star of Billy's show for the duration of the Fair. Her reputation backstroked down to Hollywood and the studios, and the next thing you knew, talent scouts with water wings were diving in the pool with her trying to get her to sign a contract with a pen that writes underwater. Esther was sure she was a swimmer, not an actress, and the best thing she could do out of water was model.

She went back to her chosen form of employment and managed to steer clear of any studio action for a year. But then a Metro-Goldwyn-Mayer representative came up with the magic formula. He offered her a contract that would ensure her a chance to study and prepare herself before facing a camera. That Esther liked, and the rest was history. Before she would go into any picture, she would train for it just as though it was the Olympics tryouts all over again.

She almost made a big splash into moviedom on the first movie they offered her. Lana Turner had run off to New York to marry Artie Shaw, and they needed a gal to replace her opposite The King, Clark Gable. Esther almost flipped her fins at the idea, but just as they were about to shoot, Lana loused things up by making a quick return. More than likely she had already received her divorce from Artie Shaw. Williams' first part was as one of Mickey Rooney's romances in *Andy Hardy's Double Life* (1942), but she felt absolutely nude because she didn't wear a bathing suit in one scene. She teamed with Red Skelton to do *Neptune's Daughter* (1949), and was billed on the billboards as "singing with Ricardo Montalban." She really could only sing underwater, so I'm sure the voice was dubbed in for her. Ricardo never 'fessed up to who did his dubbing. Again the billboards announced, "In *Take Me Out To The Ball Game* [1949] she sings with Sinatra and dances with Gene Kelly," but I'll bet they would both plead the Fifth Amendment if they were forced to say it was actually Esther Williams. Her forte was swimming, and when she jumped into those movie pools and swam toward you underwater with that beautiful smile, you were tempted to take the pledge and give up drinking booze and concentrate on that luscious H20.

WWII

In the old days of Hollywood, the movie and radio studios, NBC, ABC and CBS were all within walking distance of the Brown Derby, so luncheons and dinners were usually jammed with celebrities. Part of the attraction was that the big advertising agency people, who represented the almighty radio sponsors, also dined at the Derby. Most of the agencies were located in the Taft and Equitable buildings at the corner of Hollywood and Vine. Everyone was so busy trying to see and be seen that they almost forgot to order lunch.

But after December 7, 1941, lunch just didn't seem all that important. On that dire day, a place that 85 percent of Americans had never even heard of would make a drastic impact on their lives. Pearl Harbor was not exactly a location in your grammar school geography book. The poor guys who had been conscripted by Uncle Sam with only the threat of being separated from their employers for one year, were now in the middle of a war. Many of them had been sent to a base they couldn't even spell—Corregidor in the Philippines. Even Hollywood, used to disasters by this time, was stunned. Troops moved in from all directions and some were immediately stationed along the U.S. coastline to discourage any further aggression by Japan.

Studio trucks, any equipment that could move the G.I.s and all studio guns and ammunition were confiscated for future war needs. Hollywood itself had one night of wartime terror when word got out that enemy planes might be flying overhead. The civilian-type soldiers manning the antiaircraft guns let fly, and for a while it seemed WWII was being fought at the corner of Hollywood and Vine. Blackouts were quickly ordered, but the only blackout the local Hollywood folks were aware of was the risqué Ken Murray variety show about military life.

Bette Davis in the film *Hollywood Canteen*

Everyone got behind the "big push" because in his or her mind, Hollywood was not all that far from where the actual fighting was being waged. For the stars, it suddenly went from being a self-serving town to a self-sacrificing town. If the locals weren't enlisting in the service, they were volunteering their efforts for the success of the defense plants that were going full blast and the selling of war bonds.

The Hollywood Canteen

The challenge to the studios was to produce some movies that would bring a little fun back into people's lives in spite of the depressing atmosphere. The toughest battle during those years was finding a location that wasn't restricted by the military.

One of the industry's biggest problems, as it was with most of the nation, was to get by with shortages. To come up with creative solutions and to keep the show on the road, a whole do-it-yourself cult came into existence. Talented technical craftsmen devised ways to cut financial corners while creating devices that would work in any given situation. Much of their inventiveness is probably still being used today.

If you were lucky enough to be stationed in or near the Hollywood area during WWII, you experienced some of the greatest entertainment and most beautiful women in the world. Going to the Guild Canteen or the Hollywood Canteen was as big a thrill as scoring your first high school touchdown. On any given night any G.I. Joe just might end up dancing with Marlene Dietrich or everyone's pin-up girl, Betty Grable. Weekends the Canteens had more sleep-ins than any Army barracks within a 500 mile radius. Hollywood Boulevard overflowed with khaki and navy uniforms that outnumbered Foreman and Clark suits 10 to 1.

Any request pertaining to the well-being or entertainment of servicemen was happily met by stars such as Bette Davis, Greer Garson, Olivia de Havilland, Fred MacMurray, Mary Pickford and Mickey Rooney—all rallied 'round the flag. This was the greatest opportunity they had to prove they were just down-to-earth folks concerned about their fellow man. If they weren't selling bonds they were raising funds to support canteens for the homesick G.I.s.

Floorshows filled with talent that would have cost a fortune to see in peacetime were an every night attraction. Danny Kaye, Red Skelton, Edgar Bergen, Eddie Cantor and George Jessel provided the laughs; Dinah Shore,

Bette Davis shows Bob Hope and Marlene Dietrich the Hollywood Canteen's Hollywood Hall of Honor where pictures of movie servicemen were on display. Miss Davis is pointing to Clark Gable, who is next to George Murphy.

Nelson Eddy and Jeanette MacDonald helped provide the music. Beautiful starlets danced the night away with lucky soldiers and sailors to the Big Bands of swingers such as Kay Kyser and Duke Ellington. If you were ever going to have the chance in your life to break bread with a real-life movie star, it would have been at the Hollywood Canteens. Likewise, the stars had the chance to be with thousands and thousands of young star-struck movie fans who might never return to families and sweethearts. Between the free dancing, the free food and lodging, and a possible kiss from a well-known actress or upcoming starlet, many a G.I. flew back to camp on another freebie—cloud nine.

While the armed forces were in town, the Hollywood Brown Derby was a big attraction but mostly as a tourist site. Even though you could get the best meal in the house for less than $2, to a young soldier probably sending his pitiful paycheck back home—eating out was strictly out. The motion picture industry, its stars, producers, directors and stage technicians, all made a united war effort and directed their prowess to raising money, soliciting blood, salvaging valuable materials and educating moviegoers on the needs

Bette Davis serves food at the Hollywood Canteen

and desires of their nation. For once, there was no script—this was strictly adlib. It was truly Hollywood's finest hour. Unfortunately, it took a national tragedy to make it come about.

The public rewarded Hollywood for their wartime dedication by setting records at the box office. As many as 85 million customers a week jammed theaters in the early '40s—and they weren't all that fussy about what was showing on the silver screen. They just wanted to be entertained and for a few precious hours drive away the dark demons of war. Unfortunately, the studios, knowing they were making money in spite of themselves, began to just turn out product and fewer and fewer classics were produced. Instead of following the romanticism that had won the hearts of audiences in the '30s, they began to make darker films; life wasn't just a bowl of cherries—there were the pits that had to be considered. In spite of the fact that the average moviegoer wanted to get away from the war, he was bombarded with war films in the theaters. Some of them, when shown in Army camps, were booed. Hollywood's version of a battle wasn't anywhere near accurate, which was a blessing for worried families back home.

EDGAR BERGEN

One of the biggest frustrations in Hollywood has always been in the search for eternal youth. Faces are lifted, bags are dropped, hairpieces are doffed at every angle, but the only one who ever beat the age rap was Charlie McCarthy—so he was no dummy! Edgar Bergen never let Charlie be any older than 14. (And when was the last time *you* were 14?)

It was no pushover for Charlie, because he found his place on Edgar's knee in 1920. What McCarthy would never 'fess up to was that his first head only cost $35 and he wouldn't have even had a body if it wasn't for Bergen making one for him. What started the whole thing was Edgar buying a 25-cent book on ventriloquism. (Yes, George, they *did* sell books for 25 cents once.) From what he read and the free lessons he got daily from a famous ventriloquist, Harry Lester, Edgar developed his unusual talent. Bergen's inspiration for Charlie McCarthy was a tough Irish newsboy he had met. Edgar's first attempts at putting words in Charlie's mouth were before high school audiences at *my* old alma mater, Lake View in Chicago. Entertaining at parties with a little magic and a lot of ventriloquism helped Edgar make his way through Northwestern University in Evanston, Illinois. With the favorable reaction he was getting from audiences, Bergen decided he would like to be an actor. The closest he got was working for a Little Theatre in Decatur where he got to play the piano before the show and during intermission. It was no big strain on his talent, because it just so happened the piano was a player piano. Vaudeville was the next big step, and Bergen and McCarthy had the chance to play Iceland, England, Sweden and Russia. The politburo loved Charlie McCarthy because they had a few blockheads of their own that he closely resembled.

After appearing at some posh supper clubs such as the Rainbow Room in Rockefeller Center, New York, Edgar started his radio career by appearing weekly on the Rudy Vallee show. By 1937, Bergen and McCarthy had their own show that was so popular they held first place in the polls for two and a half years. Charlie received, would you believe, a wooden "Oscar" after the duo appeared in the $2 million dollar musical, *The Goldwyn Follies* (1938). The Motion Picture Academy made the award for the "outstanding comedy creation of 1938."

Edgar always claimed the "art of ventriloquism" was merely that of cultivating a "grunt." However, I have been in many a restaurant where some guy was cultivating a "grunt" and he didn't even have an idea what a ventriloquist was. Bergen wrote an article in the *Encyclopedia Britannica*

where he said, "You speak from the stomach instead of the throat. [*My stomach only growls!*] The tongue and the roof of the mouth substitute for the lips."

Edgar introduced Mortimer Snerd, who was an instant hit, so he decided to introduce his first female in the act, Miss Effie Klinker. But Charlie McCarthy was still the No. 1 boy in both Edgar's and the public's eyes. He had often been described as lethally precocious and irreverent, but with Bergen's clever lines coming out between Charlie's beautiful teeth (I often wondered if they were capped), you just couldn't learn to dislike this fresh kid. Edgar Bergen always said, "My appearance anyplace without Charlie was a complete failure. I do think it was a case of the tail wags the dog."

ERNEST BORGNINE

Sometimes when an actor auditions for a part he becomes very emotional, but when he finishes his reading and looks up and sees the author of the script sitting there with tears streaming down his face, the actor could cry—for joy! This is what happened to Ernest Borgnine when he had the opportunity to read the part of *Marty* for the author Paddy Chayefsky. Ernest was working on location making *Bad Day at Black Rock*, when Paddy and the producer of *Marty* flew up to give Ernie a whack at the task. Borgnine had seen the script and wanted the role so badly he could taste it. He stormed into his quarters (the scene of the audition), threw off his costume cowboy hat and started to read. The consensus was he was coming across "too Western," so Paddy calmed him down and Borgnine gave it a little more thought along with a few prayers. When he did the second reading, he was *Marty*, no doubt about it. He not only sewed up the part but he walked off with an Oscar as best actor when the film was released in 1955. Borgnine's portrayal of an overweight, lonely butcher who falls in love with a spinster schoolteacher made the picture an artistic as well as financial success. It was one of the few instances that a movie being shown at the Cannes Film Festival was interrupted seven times by the cheers and applause of the audience.

Up until the day he got the break in *Marty*, Borgnine had spent most of his time playing the role of a bad guy. A switch came for him when he took on the role of Fatso, the brutal Sergeant in charge of the stockade in *From Here to Eternity*. It wasn't easy for him to put on that Army uniform when just eight years previously he had completed a 10-year stint in the U.S. Navy. It was the good ole G.I. Bill that got him into a dramatic school, which was the springboard for his illustrious career. Until that enrollment, he hadn't given the theatrical world a second thought. Once he discovered that all villains don't get hisses—they sometimes get ovations, he knit his brows and headed in that direction. A little terrorizing, leering, and murdering never hurt anybody as long as it stayed up on that big, make-believe screen, so he made the most of it. The funny part of it is, off the screen, he's one of the nicest guys around Tinsel Town.

As is usual, the camera doesn't do him any favors as far as his weight is concerned because he photographs much heavier than he actually looks in person (and how many times have you blamed your poor Kodak for those nasty pounds that show up in those dumb snapshots of you!)

RAY BRADBURY

Being a "stargazer" outside of the Hollywood Brown Derby was a very ordinary hobby—or profession. One person who in his youth used to stand outside nightly and wait to see what celebrity would emerge, little realized that in the future some autograph seeker might be standing outside a restaurant or theater waiting for him to exit. That would be Ray Bradbury, and when I drew him he was thrilled at the idea of ending up on the wall mingling with those famous people he used to wait for on the sidewalk to try to grab a quick autograph.

One of his most exciting memories, he told me, was of the night George Raft stepped out of the Derby. It was quite late, and Ray and his young girlfriend were stranded for streetcar transportation. Raft asked them if they had a way home and when they admitted their plight, George drove them to the nearest red car that was still running and could get them to within walking distance of their home. That wasn't Science Fantasy but it sure was Filmland Fantasy.

Bradbury sailed into the science-fiction field when he was at Los Angeles High School. He had been writing since he was 12, but in high school he zeroed in on a profession when he wrote and published a magazine, *Futura Fantasia*. Unfortunately, his roommates weren't interested in the "futura," so the mag only lasted four issues. In his early life, Ray spent a year and a half with a Little Theatre Group, but that convinced him he was no actor. (I could name a lot of others who should have thought the same thing.) Like anyone with a talent, Ray was stimulated by his ability to write. Bradbury said, "I stopped reading fantasy when I began to write, because I wanted to bring back to science fiction something fresh and new." As a result, he became one of the most important names in both fantasy and science fiction today and is nationally recognized.

In this way, he admitted there was a difference between science fiction and fantasy. "If you have a leprechaun or a dinosaur appear on the streets of New York, that's improbable fantasy. But science fiction is a logical or mathematical projection of reality."

Another novelist once wrote, "Ray Bradbury has a very great and unusual talent." His wonderful writing for both the movies and books has proven that. I have my doubts they'll say that about me when this book is published.

GENE AUTRY

You've really got to love baseball if you can't play on the team—so you buy it! Such was the case of Gene Autry, whose longing was to be the number one baseball player in the country but he had to settle for being the number one movie cowboy singing star in the world. He really should have given that some thought because as a ballplayer he would have just had to sign a few autographs, but as a movie star he had to answer as many as 80,000 fan letters...a month! That is just about three times as many as other stars would receive.

If you're going to be a real cowboy you just gotta be born in Texas and Gene was—in a town called Tioga.

He did his very first singing at the age of five in his father's Baptist choir—and I'll guarantee you the song wasn't *Rudolph the Red-Nosed Reindeer*. He interrupted his singing long enough to play on a semi-pro baseball team for a short time, but he really started to earn his keep by singing in local social clubs. While he was in his teens, he became a ballad singer for the Fields Bros. Marvelous Medicine Show for the smart sum of $15 a week. You couldn't even buy a bottle of castor oil for that today. That heavy salary enabled him to buy a saxophone, but he found it very difficult to sing with that sax reed in his mouth, so he traded it for a "git-tar." The hunt and peck system was good enough to at least accompany him through a vocal. His constant singing cost him some Texas cowhand jobs because he was always being accused of distracting the other cowboys—to say nothing of the cows. There are very few moo-moos who have a good ear for music anyhow.

He got his first radio job on station KVOO, Tulsa, singing and telling stories. Gene didn't get paid anything but he did get a big title—Oklahoma's Yodeling Cowboy. You can sing all you want to, but somewhere along the line you've got to eat, so Autry took a job on the railroad. He was developing right along in songwriting by this time, so he and the train dispatcher (shows you how busy he was) collaborated on a song, "That Silver-Haired Daddy of Mine." There must have been a lot of silver-haired Daddys around who thought the song was written for them, because it sold 30,000 copies the first month and by the year 1940, had sold five million. It holds the all-time sales record for discs bought through the Sears mail-order house. So it just goes to show, if you're a frustrated songwriter, get your terrific tune sold in the Sears catalogue. It's bound to be a hit if the lyrics are tied in with batteries, refrigerators or washing machines.

Sears was so pleased with Gene's singing and all the money they were making from the sales of his record, they hired him to sing on the station they owned in Chicago, WLS. This put Gene in the big time because they offered him $35 a week. When WLS was sold to a national network, Autry stayed on and became a nation radio performer. His popularity was beginning to mount because when he went on tour with the National Barn Dance, he was the one entertainer who was besieged for autographs. This kind of recognition just had to lead to Hollywood, and Autry was selected by Republic Studios to

depict a brand-new type of cowboy—one who could sing soothing melodies instead of punching out the villain. What Republic didn't realize was that Gene Autry was the kids' favorite cowboy, and to see their hero giving that girl a yucky, smoochie kiss at the end of every picture wasn't going to get it. So Republic told Gene to save his kisses for his wife and forget that good-looking doll who was playing opposite him.

Autry wasn't the only one in his films who was getting fan mail. His horse, Champion, was also getting his fair share—more than likely from all the filly film fans. It was Gene's penchant to portray the model cowboy as a true American who always kept his acts and his actions honorable. The big cities were still too blasé to accept cowboy pictures, so Autry was unknown to them as a movie star, but in the West and the Southwest his pictures set attendance records that were only broken by his next picture.

In 1937 and 1938 he made guest appearances on Eddie Cantor's and Rudy Vallee's radio shows, which were two of the biggest on the air. Rudy would have loaned him his megaphone, but Gene couldn't hold it and play the guitar at the same time.

One of his biggest thrills happened in 1939 when he went to Dublin in the British Isles accompanied by an air-conditioned trailer housing Champion and another horse. There was such an overwhelming crowd that had turned out to greet him in O'Connell Square, he was unable to reach the theater because of the traffic jam. They probably all turned out because they thought a yodeling cowboy was a new kind of Irish whiskey being introduced. This was all taking place at the height of Gene's popularity, as theater exhibitors had voted him as the top cowboy star of 1937, 1938 and 1939. In 1940 he was acclaimed as one of the top 10 box office leaders after Clark Gable, Spencer Tracy and Mickey Rooney. Berwyn, Oklahoma was so impressed by this man, the whole population of 227 decided to change the name of their town to "Gene Autry" (and how many stars can say that!).

Royalties were rolling in from commercial products that ranged all the way from cap pistols to shaving cream all bearing his name. It was while Gene was assigned to the Army Air Forces in WWII that he took flying lessons between entertainment stints for his fellow troops. He won his wings and was transferred to the Air Transport Command, where he piloted cargo-carrying C-47s to Europe, China, Burma and the South Pacific. He returned to the South Pacific even while on terminal leave, to join a USO camp show. None of his luster as "The Cowboy" had diminished, because after he was presented with his discharge papers, his fan mail jumped to 248,000 letters, which you know is even more than "Dear Abby" gets.

TV DAZE

Beginning in the late 1940s and early 1950s, television took up where the movies left off. The number one show for years, *What's My Line?* was a sit-down panel show. Every talkie-type show that followed had a sit-down panel. *Twenty-One* had a guy groveling for answers in a telephone booth-type box. From then on, every question and answer show had someone squirming in a box trying to come up with the right word. In today's market, one sitcom show succeeds and everybody copies it (reality anyone?). Imitations are Rich Little's personal property. Whatever happened to the idea men who were supposed to have taken over this town?

While those who would be king know-it-alls were playing charades with the sagging movie business, a hurricane by the name of television was rapidly gaining popularity. Moviemakers, who had been forced to evacuate their studio locations by the invention of smog, were now being asked to step aside by this fresh kid with an antenna for a head. They had noticed him standing in the background, but with that funny little screen for a face and no expression on it but old, old movies, who could take this mechanical monstrosity seriously? Whether they liked it or not, TV was here to stay. In less than five years more than 32 million movie ticket buyers had removed themselves from the local theater and plunked themselves down on the couch in front of their own silver screen. The studios that didn't have oil wells on their lots began to panic. Studio locations quickly became real estate parcels for the development of housing and commercial units.

The plush days of the Glamour Capital of the World appeared to be disappearing with the onslaught of the television demon. Only one big studio, Paramount, had poised itself for what was taking place. Somebody up there in

Beryl Wallace and Earl Carroll died in a plane crash in 1948

My contribution to TV—"Jack-Add-A-Line Lane"

their front office must have had an idea of what an impact TV would make, so they brought in Klaus Landsberg to establish the first commercial television station west of Chicago, KTLA. Landsberg's initial big endeavor was to present a Saturday night program called *The Beryl Wallace Show*, and if you didn't like watching that one, you went to bed early, because that was it on a Saturday night. Beryl was Earl Carroll's girlfriend at the time, which were her credentials for having the big, big show on a small, small station. For the performers it was a "freebie," but then everyone wanted exposure.

Not the kind of "exposure" you see on movie screens today, but the kind of exposure where you could say "Hey, look at me. I'm on TV!" This was before they had all the nudniks waving at the camera hysterically and hollering "Hi mom!" "Send money, Pop!" or "Give 'em hell, Howard Cosell!"

Numbered among the frustrated performers appearing on the show was a very funny guy working with a partner doing pantomime to records, namely Dick Van Dyke. Need I tell you where Dick went from the spawning grounds of that show?

My contribution to the proceedings was to open the show by drawing a few lines of a potential personality on my easel and the show would then

Francis X. Bushman faces my pen on live TV in the 1950s.

segue into the first act. I was known as "Jack-Add-A-Line Lane," so I would come back several times throughout the show and add some lines to tease the viewer into coming up with an identification. I'll have you know that even back then, they offered big glamorous prizes. If you called in before I completed the drawing and correctly identified the celeb, you won a watch—a genuine $10 timekeeper with a second hand, a crystal face and a winder, yet! The studio (or should I say "cave") had a switchboard with one, that's right folks, one incoming line.

That was probably the birth of the pro contestants who dialed all the numbers but the last digit and then, as soon as I lay my hand on the board, they let the last number fly and hoped they had the correct answer if they got through to the operator.

The real fun for me was the night after the show when stars like Eddie Cantor, Phil Harris and Alice Faye would tap me on the shoulder as I sat at the Brown Derby drawing somebody and say, "As soon as you drew that first line, I knew who it was going to be. We tried to call, but we couldn't get through. But it was that first line!" I appreciated their enthusiasm, but I had that thing so rehearsed that even I didn't know who it was going to be until

I was halfway through. It would only be a wild guess if it was any sooner, and once you got through guessing Bob Hope or Jimmy Durante, and it was wrong, then you had a game on your hands.

Several years later, I had two television game show writers come to my home with a "sensational idea" for a TV show. It was to be called *Dotto*. I'm sure that rings a bell for you, because that show had some kind of a case history. Their big idea turned out to be exactly what I had been doing on TV, only with numbers. *Dotto* consisted of figuring out a sequence of numbers that, when you followed through in rotation, you would be creating a face of some well-known personality. Now that was a grinder. First, I had to convince them you couldn't possibly draw a straight line, as a kid does, in a numbers cartoon book. The line from one through six had to flow a little, so you could get the shape of a nose or a mouth out of it. On top of that, the way they had it figured, the artist would sit unseen behind the paper with the numbers and when the contestant answered another 10-point question correctly, the audience would see a mysterious black line showing up between numbers 1 through 10.

We went through all the rituals and the headaches of babying this thing up to the pilot stage. Now the pilot is sold to who else, a big soap company, and the dickering starts for me. The show is to be done in New York. I had three kids in school in California, and I couldn't envision hauling up stakes and selling the house, just to get mugged walking to the studio some night in the Big Apple. I offered to create the dot drawings here and ship them back there, but that idea didn't thrill them. In hindsight, it was the luck of the Irish that prevailed for me.

If you recall, it was that particular show where the standby contestant saw the producer talking to "Everybody's Favorite" contestant who had been on for many days building his winnings into a fortune. The producer handed him a slip of paper and when the call came, "Everybody on the set," the egghead put the paper down and walked onto the set. A standby picked up the paper and saw all the correct answers to that day's telecast. Nuff said? First, he tried blackmailing the producers and, when that didn't work, he went to the district attorney and blew the whistle. Immediately, every question and answer show became highly suspect and *Dotto* was responsible for the bombing of *$64,000 Question*

and several others. That was one sinking ship I deserted just in time.

By the mid 1950s and '60s, TV had roared past the motion picture industry in popularity. Facing up to it, the film companies realized they had blown the opportunity to adopt television as their foster kid and like any good father or mother, mold it into a parent's image. With their practical know-how by this time, it would have been a cinch to make television another branch of the movie business. Because of the film genius' shortsightedness, the networks had taken over and the best the studios could do was to rent space to them to produce their own products.

LOCAL

Artist's caricatures come back to life

Jack Lane maintains a gallery of the celebrity caricatures he did for the Brown Derby in the studio of his hilltop Woodland Hills home.

THAT'S A WRAP

So as not to cause you any undue alarm as to my artistic ability, I wish to remind you that many of these caricatures were done as much as 55 years ago. In the meantime, something happened to my victims, which happens to the best of us. A thing called age sneaked up and clobbered them. Where you used to see one, such as in "chin," you now see two. The hair that was black has now seceded or receded, and what's left of it has a gray that in many cases matches the complexion. However, if you think *they* look bad, when you shave tomorrow, be sure to look in that mirror head on and don't lie to yourself.

The Hollywood Brown Derby tipped its hat good-bye to Vine Street in 1987 after a long hard run. The third and last owner tried to open several other locations using the title, "The Brown Derby," and I still drew celebs in those places until the bitter end in 1993.

I keep my show on the road by sketching caricatures from photographs of retiring Presidents of the Rotary and Kiwanis Clubs nationwide each year. However as I tell everyone—the last people on this earth I'm going to draw will be my pallbearers. If they throw my pencil in the box and I don't pick it up, they know I'm gone!

I'm still drawing and currently I am looking for syndication for my cartoon strip.

At Midnight Marquee We Know Movies!

Visit www.midmar.com
for a complete listing of books
from Midnight Marquee Press, Inc.

or write for a free catalog to:
Midnight Marquee Press, Inc.
9721 Britinay Lane
Baltimore, MD 21234

410-665-1198

www.ingramcontent.com/pod-product-compliance
Lightning Source LLC
Chambersburg PA
CBHW071439080526
44587CB00014B/1909